East of the Sun

TEACHER'S EDITION
LEVEL 5

ODYSSEY An HBJ Literature Program

Sam Leaton Sebesta, General Consultant

Star Light, Star Bright
Hello and Good-bye
Where the Clouds Go
The Heart of the Woods

Under the Midnight Stars
Across Wide Fields
East of the Sun

At the Edge of the World
Ride the Silver Seas
Another Earth, Another Sky

 Harcourt Brace Jovanovich, Publishers
New York   Chicago   San Francisco   Atlanta   Dallas   *and*   London

Printed in the United States of America

ISBN 0-15-333366-9

We do not include a Teacher's Edition automatically with each shipment of a classroom set of textbooks. We prefer to send a Teacher's Edition only when requested by the teacher or administrator concerned or by one of our representatives. A Teacher's Edition can be easily mislaid when it arrives as part of a shipment delivered to a school stockroom, and, since it contains answer materials, we want to be sure it is sent *directly* to the person who will use it or to someone concerned with the use or selection of textbooks.

If your classroom assignment changes and you no longer are using or examining this Teacher's Edition, you may wish to pass it on to a teacher who will be using it.

Acknowledgments

The publisher gratefully acknowledges the contributions of Peder Jones and Phyllis Goldenberg to the preparation of the Teacher's Edition lessons.

For permission to reprint copyrighted material, grateful acknowledgment is made to the following sources:

The Bodley Head: From "Echo and Narcissus" in *Tales the Muses Told* by Roger Lancelyn Green. Copyright © 1965 by Roger Lancelyn Green.

The Book House for Children, Lake Bluff, Illinois: From "East O' the Sun and West O' the Moon" from *The Magic Garden of My Book House* (Vol. 7) by Olive Beaupre Miller, editor.

Coward, McCann & Geoghegan, Inc.: Adapted from *Where Was Patrick Henry on the 29th of May?* by Jean Fritz. Text copyright © 1975 by Jean Fritz.

The Dial Press: "I never asked for no allergy" excerpted from the book *Philip Hall Likes Me. I Reckon Maybe* by Bette Greene. Copyright © 1974 by Bette Greene.

E. P. Dutton: From "Bando" (retitled) from *My Side of the Mountain* by Jean George. Copyright © 1959 by Jean George.

Farrar, Straus and Giroux, Inc.: From "The Megrimum" (retitled) from *Kneeknock Rise* by Natalie Babbitt. Copyright © 1970 by Natalie Babbitt.

Harcourt Brace Jovanovich, Inc.: From "The Big Wind of '34" abridged from *Grandpa's Farm,* © 1965 by James Flora.

Harper & Row, Publishers, Inc.: Specified excerpt from p. 27 in *The Odyssey of Homer,* translated by Richmond Lattimore. Copyright © 1965, 1967 by Richmond Lattimore. Specified excerpt from *A Tree Grows in Brooklyn* by Betty Smith. Copyright, 1943, by Betty Smith.

Macmillan Publishing Co., Inc.: "Mix a Pancake" from *Sing-Song* by Christina G. Rossetti. Macmillan Publishing Co., Inc., 1924.

David McKay Co., Inc. and Mrs. Helen Thurber: From *Plays and How to Put Them On* by Moyne Rice Smith. © 1961 by Moyne Rice Smith. Published by Henry Z. Walck, Inc. Based on the book *The Great Quillow* by James Thurber, published by Harcourt Brace Jovanovich, Inc. Copyright © 1944 by James Thurber. Copyright © 1972 by Helen W. Thurber.

Eve Merriam: Excerpt from "Thumbprint" from *It Doesn't Always Have to Rhyme* by Eve Merriam. Copyright © 1964 by Eve Merriam.

Robert Lescher Literary Agency, Inc.: Quotes by Isaac Bashevis Singer.

Russell & Volkening, Inc. as agent for the author: From "A Wagon Load of Bricks" in *Harriet Tubman: Conductor on the Underground Railroad* by Ann Petry. Copyright © 1955 by Ann Petry.

Scholastic Magazines, Inc.: From *The Crane Maiden* by Miyoko Matsutani. Text copyright © 1968 by Parents' Magazine Press.

Frederick Warne & Company, Inc.: From "The Jumblies" by Edward Lear.

Contents

Introduction to ODYSSEY   T20

Thematic Strands in ODYSSEY   T24

Skills Index for Level 5   T26

Teaching Literature in the Classroom
    Sam Leaton Sebesta   T32

Poetry and the Teacher   Myra Cohn Livingston   T50

Folk Literature and the Teacher   Barre Toelken   T54

Resource Center   T57

1 It Must Be a Trick   13

2 Truly Amazing Talents   69

3 Never Give Up   149

4 Facing the Unknown   215

5 To Live with Nature   297

6 From America's Past   361

Glossary   413

General Consultant

Sam Leaton Sebesta is on the faculty of the University of Washington in Seattle, where he teaches reading and children's literature. A former elementary grade teacher, Dr. Sebesta has written numerous books and articles in the field of reading, and has earned national recognition for his speeches and workshops on teaching literature. From 1975 to 1979 he was a regional coordinator for Classroom Choices, a joint project of the Children's Book Council and the International Reading Association. Dr. Sebesta received his doctorate from Stanford University.

Consultants

Elaine M. Aoki is an administrator and reading specialist for the Seattle, Washington, public schools and was formerly an elementary school teacher in Auburn, Washington. She received her doctorate in reading from the University of Washington.

Willard E. Bill is an assistant professor and Director of the Indian Teacher Education Program at the University of Washington.

Sylvia Engdahl is an anthologist and author of science fiction and nonfiction for young people. She has written numerous articles on children's literature and is best known for her novel *Enchantress from the Stars,* a Newbery Honor Book.

Carolyn Horovitz is a former librarian in the Santa Monica, California, public schools and the University Elementary School at UCLA. She is the editor of the *Anthology of Children's Literature* (5th ed.) and a past member of the Newbery and Caldecott awards committees.

Daphne P. Muse is a lecturer in children's literature at Mills College in Oakland, California, and a children's book reviewer for KGO-TV (ABC).

Margaret D. Simpson is a specialist in children's books and Director of the Story Theatre Program for the Albany, California, public schools.

Consulting Educators

Sonya Blackman is an assistant manager of the Books Unlimited Cooperative and an instructor in children's literature at the University of California Extension in Berkeley. She received her master's degree in early childhood education from Sonoma State University.

Myra Cohn Livingston is an author and award-winning poet. She is Poet-in-Residence and a teacher of creative writing for the Beverly Hills Unified School District and is a Senior Instructor at the UCLA Extension.

Barre Toelken is a professor of English and Director of the Ethnic Studies Program at the University of Oregon, Eugene, Oregon. Dr. Toelken is a past president of the American Folklore Society and a former editor of the *Journal of American Folklore.*

William Anderson
Department of English
California State University
  at Northridge
Northridge, California

Gwen Batey
Teacher
William F. Turnbull Middle
  School
San Mateo, California

Dorothy W. Blake
Coordinator of Planning for
  Media Resources and
  Utilization
Division of Instructional
  Planning and Development
Atlanta Public Schools
Atlanta, Georgia

Carlota Cardenas de Dwyer
Department of English
The University of Texas
  at Austin
Austin, Texas

John M. Chavez
Educational Consultant
The Urban Institute for Human
  Services, Inc.
San Francisco, California

Joan Cheifetz
Principal
Thornhill School
Oakland Unified School District
Oakland, California

Ann Cheleen
Teacher
H. O. Sonnesyn Elementary
  School
New Hope, Minnesota

Harold Fenderson
Principal
R. V. Daniels Elementary
  School
Jacksonville, Florida

Barbara Friedberg
Teacher
Martin Luther King, Jr.,
  Laboratory School
Evanston, Illinois

M. Jean Greenlaw
College of Education
North Texas State University
Denton, Texas

Elsa Konig Heald
Teacher
Sun Valley Elementary School
San Rafael, California

Franklin Koontz
Teacher
Bellevue School District
Bellevue, Washington

Joanne Lincoln
Librarian, Professional Library
Atlanta Public Schools
Atlanta, Georgia

Frances Mackie
Teacher
Detroit Public Schools
Detroit, Michigan

Richard McBreen
Teacher
William F. Turnbull Middle
  School
San Mateo, California

Nancy Lofton Morrow
Teacher, retired
Carmel Valley, California

Evelyn Myton-Plantillas
Resource Specialist
San Jose Unified School
  District
San Jose, California

E. Renee Nathan
Director of Curriculum and
  Special Projects, K-12
Lodi Unified School District
Lodi, California

Ben Nelms
Department of English and
  College of Education
University of Missouri
Columbia, Missouri

Elizabeth Nelms
Teacher
Hickman High School
Columbia, Missouri

Soledad P. Newman
Department of English
Miami University
Oxford, Ohio

Kay Palmer
Teacher
Shoreline School District
Shoreline, Washington

Barbara K. Rand
Teacher
Springfield Middle School
Springfield, Pennsylvania

Beverly Remer
Teacher
New York City Public Schools
District 10
New York, New York

Doris Shriber
Teacher
William F. Turnbull Middle
  School
San Mateo, California

Barbara M. Shulgold
Teacher
Vallemar Structured School
Pacifica, California

Clarice Stafford
Assistant Superintendent for
  Curriculum
Wayne-Westland Schools
Wayne, Michigan

Barbara Tapolow
Teacher
P.S. 124
New York, New York

Ann Terry
School of Professional
  Education
University of Houston at Clear
  Lake City
Houston, Texas

Kelley Tucker
Teacher
Sun Valley Elementary School
San Rafael, California

Lois Wendt
Teacher
Crystal Heights School
Crystal, Minnesota

ODYSSEY

An HBJ Literature Program, Levels 1-8

odyssey (ăd′ ə sē) *n.* A long wandering journey. Your students travel to new places, meet new characters, and discover new insights that deepen their sense of themselves and expand their view of the world…in a word, ODYSSEY. It's an adventure in memorable experiences, an introduction to the riches of the imagination.

In every level, ODYSSEY presents an exceptional variety of quality literature, written by an outstanding selection of classic and contemporary writers.

From Level 1 to Level 8, ODYSSEY will help you inspire your students to read and enjoy literature. ODYSSEY also offers students a solid foundation in literary appreciation and helps build skills in reading, writing, speaking, and listening.

Features of ODYSSEY

• High-interest poems, plays, short stories, science fiction, folk tales, excerpts from biographies and novels, essays, and more.

• Writers who represent the diversity of our society, including E.B. White, Beverly Cleary, Ernesto Galarza, Jamake Highwater, Virginia Hamilton, Laurence Yep, Nicholasa Mohr.

• Dazzling art that enhances each selection.

• A range of reading levels that will appeal to students of various reading abilities.

• A thematic structure that focuses on relationships, adventure, humor, fantasy, and more.

• Skill-building material students can use on their own.

• Student-centered activities that develop literary understanding and appreciation.

Turn the page to see samples of the features you'll find in ODYSSEY.

Here are some examples of the

Mix a Pancake

A poem by Christina Rossetti

Mix a pancake,
Stir a pancake,
    Pop it in the pan;
Fry the pancake,
Toss the pancake,—
    Catch it if you can.

Your students will enjoy reading the stories, plays, poems, and songs. In ODYSSEY, every student will find selections of interest and appeal.

In every book, students will read selections by award-winning authors— Maurice Sendak, Lucille Clifton, C.S. Lewis, Arnold Lobel, Karla Kuskin, E.L. Konigsburg, Langston Hughes, Taro Yashima, Natalie Babbitt, Laura Ingalls Wilder.

The Big Wind of '34

A tall tale by James Flora
Pictures by Marie-Louise Gay

If you stay around Grandpa long enough, you will hear all sorts of amazing stories about his farm. Some people might call them tall tales, but you can decide for yourself after reading this tale as Grandpa tells it.

When Grandma and I first came to the farm, there was no barn—just a house. We were very poor and couldn't afford to build a barn. We had a cow, and she had to sleep outside. She didn't like that at all. On cold days she would get so angry that she wouldn't give us any milk.

265

Pages reduced. Actual size 7½" x 9".

variety you'll find in ODYSSEY

Throughout ODYSSEY, your students will discover authors and illustrators whose ideas and imagery invite their readers back for more.

From Level 5

The Great Quillow
A play by Moyne Rice Smith
based on the story by James Thurber
Illustrated by Sal Murdocca

Characters

Lamplighter	
Town Crier	Baker
Town Clerk	Candlemaker
Blacksmith	Cobbler
Tailor	Carpenter
Butcher	Locksmith
Candymaker	Quillow, the Toymaker
	Hunder, the Giant

Setting: Village square.
Time: Many years ago.

The village clock strikes seven. Lamplighter enters with his long staff and lights the street lamp.

Hunder sits above our village and curses it. What can we do? He has plundered the villages of the far countryside. And today the earth shook when he strode onto our hillside. He

From Level 8

A Wagon Load of Bricks
A chapter from the biography *Harriet Tubman: Conductor on the Underground Railroad* by Ann Petry
Illustrated by Kenneth Longtemps

Harriet Tubman was a great leader in the fight against slavery in America. Born a slave in Maryland, she ran away and made the dangerous journey North in 1849, when she was twenty-nine. She returned South to conduct other slaves to freedom along the Underground Railroad. Her courage has inspired many writers, like Ann Petry who wrote the biography from which this excerpt is taken. Another such writer is Hildegarde Hoyt Swift, who wrote the following verse as part of a longer poem entitled "I brought to the New World the gift of devotion."

> I was Harriet Tubman, who would not stay in bondage.
> I followed the devious, uncharted trails to the North,
> I followed the light of the North Star,
>   I ran away to freedom in 1849.
> I was Harriet Tubman who could not stay in freedom,
>   While her brothers were enslaved.
> . . . .
>   I was Harriet Tubman,
>   Who "never run my train off the track,
>   And never lost a passenger."

FROM 1851 TO 1857, the country moved closer to civil war. During these years Harriet Tubman made eleven trips into Maryland to bring out slaves.

In November, 1856, she rescued Joe Bailey. In the spring she had made two trips to the Eastern Sh.... result of one of these tri....

266

T9

Here are more stimulating

Illustrations will help your students visualize story characters, settings, and actions, making literature a more enjoyable experience.

BANDO

From the novel *My Side of the Mountain*
by Jean Craighead George
Illustrated by Lyle Miller

It was late spring when Sam Gribley left his family's crowded New York City apartment home and set out for some land in the Catskill Mountains that his great-grandfather had once tried to farm. He carried only a penknife, a ball of string, an ax, a flint with steel,[1] and forty dollars. He knew how to fish and build fires, and he figured that was all he needed for a new life.

During his first few days in the wilds, Sam was

The Crane Maiden

A Japanese folk tale retold by Miyoko Matsutani
English version by Alvin Tresselt
Illustrated by Masami Miyamoto

Long years ago, at the edge of a small mountain village in the snow country of Japan, there lived an old man and his wife. They had little in this world that they could call their own. But they were happy in their life together.

Now one winter morning the old man set out for the village with a bundle of firewood fastened to his back. It was bitter cold. He knew he would have little trouble selling the wood. Then with the money, he would buy some food so that he and his wife could have a good supper.

As the old man trudged through the falling snow, he was suddenly aware of a fluttering sound, and a pitiful cry of *Koh, koh*. Turning from the path to investigate, he came upon a great crane frantically trying to free herself from a trap.

The old man's heart was touched with pity for the magnificent bird. While he tried to soothe the crane with tender words, his hands released the cruel spring of the trap. At once the crane flew up, joyfully calling *Koh, koh*, and disappeared into the snowy sky.

T10

93

selections from ODYSSEY

In Levels 1 and 2, wordless picture stories develop visual literacy. By reading and retelling picture stories, students increase their oral vocabulary and their ability to find meaning and "a sense of story" in pictures.

Your students will find units on fantasy, humor, and the natural world throughout the books. In Levels 5 and 8, special units focus on the people, heroes, and events in America's past. Level 7 includes a unit on myths and epics. These thematic units will help you enrich the various curriculum areas you teach.

ECHO & NARCISSUS

A GREEK MYTH RETOLD BY ROGER LANCELYN GREEN
ILLUSTRATED BY KATIE THAMER

The gods took a devilish delight in punishment. When someone angered one of them—and the gods were quick to take offense—the offender was tortured in a way that cleverly fit the crime. The goddess Hera, who was forever tracking down her flirtatious husband, Zeus, became particularly skilled at punishing his sweethearts. She changed one beautiful maid into a hairy bear. When Zeus tried to disguise another girl friend as a cow, Hera had a gadfly pursue the cow around the earth. Now the beautiful nymph Echo is about to feel Hera's wrath.

U P ON THE WILD, lonely mountains of Greece lived the Oreades,[1] the nymphs or fairies of the hills, and among them one of the most beautiful was called Echo. She was one of the most talkative, too, and once she talked too much and angered Hera, wife of Zeus, king of the gods.

When Zeus grew tired of the golden halls of Mount Olympus, the home of the immortal gods, he would come down to earth and wander with the nymphs on the mountains. Hera, however, was jealous and often came to see what he was doing. It seemed strange at first that she always met Echo, and that Echo kept her listening for hours on end to her stories and her gossip.

But at last Hera realized that Echo was doing this on purpose to detain her while Zeus went quietly back to Olympus as if he had never really been away.

"So nothing can stop you talking?" exclaimed Hera. "Well, Echo, I do not intend to spoil your pleasure. But from this

1. Oreades (OHR • ee • AH] • eez)

T11

Special features develop literary

Learn About Literature features help students develop an appreciation for literature and an understanding of various literary elements and devices. Students learn about such literary elements as setting, plot, and characterization. They learn to use such literary devices as rhythm, repetition, and figurative language. They become aware of illustration styles, uses of the library, and more.

Literary excerpts and examples are used to help students learn about specific aspects of literature. And activities provide opportunities for students to practice what they are learning.

Learn About
Libraries
Animals in the Library

These books are all mixed up. Some are storybooks. Some are fact books. Can you help me get the books on the right shelves?

I'll find the storybooks.

I'll find the fact books.

Storybooks

Fact Books

From Level 5

Learn About
Stories

Characters to Remember

Think about some favorite characters in stories you have read. Were they brave? determined? clever? honest? wicked? These are all *traits*. A character's traits are what make that character stand out in your mind. They are what make a character someone you are likely to remember.

A character's traits may be learned from what that character says. What traits do you detect in Beth from what she says in the following section from the story "I Never Asked for No Allergy"? In this scene, Beth is saying good-bye to her dog, Friendly, because she is allergic to him.

At the kennel I held Friendly close to me while Pa explained about the allergy to Mr. Grant. "You are welcome to swap," he said, reaching out for Friendly.

"Wait!" I said. "A person has got to say good-bye, don't they?" I looked into Friendly's eyes and wondered how I could make him understand. "I never wanted to get rid of you, Friendly. I only wanted to get rid of the aller—*Her-her-choo!*—of the allergy."

Caring, sensitive, concerned—these are traits you may have observed in Beth from what she says.

A character's traits also may be learned from what the author tells us. Here is the way author Natalie Babbitt describes Egan as he begins to climb the mountain in the story "The Megrimum."

. . . Egan was half an hour ahead by that time. And he was young and strong, alone—and determined.

Later in that story, the traits of being *strong* and *determined* are shown in what Egan does—in his actions.

Egan, deep in the mist, heard nothing. He wandered up the final stony slope toward the top like a sleepwalker lost in dreams. . . . And then he stopped, chilled suddenly out of his trance. Just ahead there came a noise as of an animal thrashing about, and the low rumble of a voice.

He crept forward, grasping the nearly forgotten stick tightly, and his heart pounded. The Megrimum! At last, the Megrimum! Slay it, perhaps—perhaps; but at least he would see it.

More thrashing in the weeds ahead. "Owanna-ooowanna," the voice seemed to murmur.

Closer and closer crept Egan and then he saw it dimly, all flailing arms, rolling about on the ground.

209

T12

understanding and appreciation

At the primary levels, *Learn About Literature* features focus on such literary elements and devices as story characters, story sequence, sound words, story structure, plots, poetry, and more.

At the intermediate levels, there are features about plays, writing quatrains (four-line poems) and limericks, figurative language, biography, characterization, and theme.

In Levels 7 and 8, these features cover a variety of topics, including writing a newspaper, performing Readers Theatre, learning about science fiction and fantasy, writing humorous essays, understanding poetry, and learning how authors use setting and point of view. There are several *Learn About Literature* features in each book at Levels 1-6, five in Level 7, and six in Level 8.

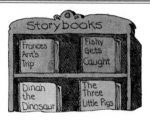

Choose a book for each animal.

I like dinosaurs. Where can I find out more about them?

I have a new pet ant. What can I feed her?

Learn About Poetry

by Myra Cohn Livingston

Artists use drawing materials and paint to make portraits, or likenesses of people. Photographers use film and cameras; poets use words.

In their portraits of people, poets present words in a special way—not to *tell* us—but to *show* us, through descriptions, details, and conversations, what a person is really like.

Alice Walker's poem "For My Sister Molly Who in the Fifties," on page 220, is a portrait of her older sister. Although there are many descriptions of what Molly does, the poet never tells us whether Molly is sad, angry, bad, or kind. We learn that Molly cooked, cleaned, answered children's questions, knew songs of Africa, and loved to read aloud. In addition she

> Knew all the written things
> that made
> Us laugh and stories by
> The hour

The poet's sister Molly

> . . . made dresses, braided
> Hair. Moved chairs about
> Hung things from walls
> Ordered baths
> Frowned on wasp bites
> And seemed to know the endings
> Of all the tales
> I had forgot.

Through her choice of details, Alice Walker gives us an idea of what *she* thinks of her sister Molly, but she allows us to decide for ourselves what *we* think.

In Leonard Adamé's poem "My Grandmother Would Rock Quietly and Hum," on page 192, the poet shows us an older woman in her house.

> She would rock quietly and hum
> until her swelled hands
> calmed
>
> in summer
> she wore thick stockings
> sweaters
> and gray braids

The poet says that

> she had lost her teeth
> and when we ate
> she had bread
> soaked in *café*
>
> always her eyes
> were clear

We see her shopping, cooking, and talking about her girlhood days. In this way Leonard Adamé shows us what his grandmother does in the same way that Alice Walker shows us the things Molly did, but Adamé gives us a physical description of his character whereas Walker does not.

When you read T. S. Eliot's poem "Macavity: The Mystery Cat," on page 148, the poet tells you immediately that Macavity is "the master criminal who can defy the Law." The poet then shows you the kind of criminal is by describing his appearance actions. It is up to you to deci Macavity *is* in fact the master and just how wicked his deeds

Many poems give us not on two portraits: one of the person the subject of the poem and ar of the speaker (or narrator). Of

244

ODYSSEY includes skill-building material students can do on their own

Questions and Activity pages foster students' critical reading and creative writing skills. You'll find this feature at the end of most prose selections to help you enhance the reading and writing skills you teach.

By including levels of questions that range from simple (recall and inference) to more complex (extrapolation and relating reading to experience), students may test their literal, interpretive, and critical reading skills. Activities provide opportunities for a range of responses, from speaking and writing, to drawing and performing.

In levels 7 and 8, special *Understanding Literature* sections along with the *Questions* and *Activities* add to students' knowledge and appreciation of various literary elements and techniques. The questions, activities, and composition assignments at these levels help students learn skills of self-expression, how to identify the theme of a story, explore the use of repetition for effect, create a story sequence, and more.

From Level 7

■ Understanding the Story

1. Miyax tries to make herself one of the pack by imitating the wolves' movements and sounds. What signal does she give Amaroq that finally makes him accept her?

2. The adult wolves in the pack are Amaroq, Silver, Nails, and Jello. Amaroq is the leader. Nails is an adult male whose status is lower than Amaroq's. What are the positions or the duties assigned to Silver and Jello?

3. The author of "One of the Pack" tells you what Miyax says and does and also what Miyax thinks and feels. In the story, find one detail to support each of these statements: Miyax is a) resourceful, b) sensitive to animals, c) courageous.

4. The old Eskimo hunters, Miyax recalls, thought that "the riches of life were intelligence, fearlessness, and love." What do you think are the riches of life?

5. Based on what you know about her from this story, what do you think Miyax will be doing in six or seven years when she is nineteen or twenty?

■ Understanding Literature

Most writers tell stories in chronological order—that is, the order in which the events happened. In "One of

the Pack," the writer stops the action to tell you what has occurred in the past. She takes you back into Miyax's past when she uses a technique called *flashback*. The scene on page 19 at Miyax's school in Barrow "last winter" is a flashback. Notice how the author returns to the events of the story after the flashback.

■ Writing About the Story

If you were working on a team that studies animal communication, you would write reports based on your observations of the animals' behavior. Choose an animal to study and take notes on what you observe. Notice the signals the animal uses to communicate with other animals and with people. Then prepare a short report for the other members of your imaginary team. For the first part of the report, use your notes to write an account of what the animal did while you observed it. Then write a paragraph which tells what signals the animal used and what you think those signals mean.

When you've finished writing, read your report carefully to make sure it will be clear to readers. You could ask a friend or parent to read it, too. Then make any changes that will improve your report.

29

Questions

1. Billy made two state[...] might be fibbing. Wh[...]

2. When did Encyclope[...] had a *problem?*

3. What did Encyclope[...] to try to *solve* the p[...]

4. Why did the author [...] story, not within it?

5. In this story, a *susp[...]
   a. is the wrongdoer[...]
   b. might be the wrongdoer.
   c. is innocent, but is accused of being the wrongdoer.

Activity

If Encyclopedia Brown had not found Sally's roller skates, he might have put an advertisement in a newspaper, offering a reward for their return. Write an advertisement for Encyclopedia. In your advertisement, tell what the skates looked like, and where and when they were last seen.

21

From Level 4

These special features will help your students appreciate literature even more

About the Author features give readers a glimpse into the lives of authors. Quotes that provide insights into the authors' ideas and techniques, and information on how authors began their careers, help students to see authors as real people.

From Level 6

About ISAAC BASHEVIS SINGER

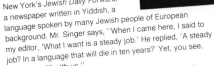

Isaac Bashevis Singer's stories are set in Jewish communities much like those he knew as a young boy growing up in Poland in the early 1900s. His father was a rabbi (a leader or teacher of the Jewish religion), and his mother was a rabbi's daughter. Although he studied to become a rabbi, Isaac Bashevis Singer found work as a journalist instead. In 1935 he came to the United States and got a job on New York's *Jewish Daily Forward,* a newspaper written in Yiddish, a language spoken by many Jewish people of European background. Mr. Singer says, ''When I came here, I said to my editor, 'What I want is a steady job.' He replied, 'A steady job? In a language that will die in ten years?' Yet, you see, Yiddish is still with us.''

Isaac Bashevis Singer continues to write his stories in Yiddish, and then supervises their translation into English. His stories, however, have been praised for their appeal to people of all cultures. In 1979 he was given the Nobel Prize for Literature, the highest honor a writer can receive.

More Books by Isaac Bashevis Singer

Zlateh the Goat and Other Stories
The Fearsome Inn
A Day of Pleasure: Stories of a Boy Growing Up in Warsaw

From Level 4

BOOKSHELF

The Ghost on Saturday Night by Sid Fleischman. Little, Brown, 1974. Opie guides a mean-looking stranger through the thick fog. His reward is two tickets to a ghost-raising. Opie doesn't know he has front-row seats to a bank robbery, too.

The Trouble with Jenny's Ear by Oliver Butterworth. Little, Brown, 1960. When Jenny hears thoughts before they are spoken, she begins to wonder what is wrong with her.

Katie John by Mary Calhoun. Harper & Row, 1960. Katie John thinks she is going to spend a boring summer in Missouri. Then a neighbor tells her that the house Katie is staying in is haunted.

A-Haunting We Will Go; Ghostly Stories and Poems collected by Lee Bennett Hopkins. Albert Whitman, 1977. Some of these ghost stories and poems will make you laugh. Some will make you shiver.

The Shrinking of Treehorn by Florence Parry Heide. Holiday House, 1971. Treehorn sees that shelves are getting higher, and his clothes are getting looser. Can he really be shrinking?

119

At the end of each textbook, Levels 4-8, definitions of important words provide independent vocabulary study.

A list of key literary terms appears at the end of each textbook, Levels 6-8. Definitions as well as examples taken from the selections help to explain the meaning and use of each literary element or device.

To encourage independent reading, *Bookshelf* provides an annotated list of books that students may read on their own for enjoyment and for further study of each unit theme. This feature appears at the end of each unit in Levels 2-8.

Annotated Teacher's Editions

Teacher's Editions provide you with all the material you need to teach each lesson: objectives, pre-reading information and suggestions, post-reading discussion questions and enrichment activities. Lessons are annotated directly on the student's pages appearing in each Teacher's Edition.

From Level 5 Teacher's Edition

Most selections have at least two objectives. Some objectives focus on literary appreciation and an understanding of literature and literary elements. Other objectives show how literature relates to human experience.

Synopses provide summaries of the main points of the story or play.

The reading level of each prose selection is designated as "easy," "average," or "challenging."

Objectives ● To enjoy a historical biography. ● To recognize how a character can influence the lives of others. ● To create a time line for a biography. ● To recognize the effect of a historical figure upon events of the time.

Synopsis of the Story As a young man, Patrick Henry failed as a farmer and as a storekeeper. He then worked in his father-in-law's tavern, where he met many lawyers. He attended court sessions and decided to practice law. After studying on his own, Patrick Henry was issued a law license. His practice was small and his reputation of little note until he won a case for the Virginia colonists against the state's parsons. During the succeeding years, Patrick Henry fought against England's unjust taxation. In 1775, his words "Give me liberty or give me death" became the rallying cry for American patriots.

From

Reading Level Challenging

Where Was Patrick Henry on the 29th of May?

362

Pages reduced. Actual size 7½" x 9".

Where appropriate, a background section provides such useful information as historical or geographical details, cultural or ethnic background, and awards won by the book or author.

Introductory material often sets the mood of each selection or relates the subject or theme to something familiar to students, establishing a purpose for reading each selection.

Key vocabulary words needed for students to understand the selection are listed. Page numbers identify the location where each word first appears.

Background In 1975, *Where Was Patrick Henry on the 29th of May?* was one of the Library of Congress Children's Books of the Year and was on the American Library Association Notable Children's Books list.

Introducing the Story *Who were some of the important leaders of the American Revolution?* (Possible answers: George Washington; Thomas Jefferson; Benjamin Franklin; Thomas Paine.) *What is each person famous for?* (Possible answers:

Washington led the American army and became President; Jefferson wrote the Declaration of Independence; Franklin served as ambassador to France; Paine wrote influential pamphlets.) *These people lived so long ago that they may not seem very real to us. You may feel differently after you read this story about Patrick Henry, one of the leaders of the American Revolution.*

Word to Know

orator: an effective speaker. (page 370)

On the 29th of May, 1736, Patrick Henry had just been born in Hanover County, Virginia. In those days, Virginia was still a colony of England and a wilderness of woodlands, creeks, and rivers. As a boy, Patrick often went off to the woods to hunt or fish. He even developed a good ear for birdcalls.

Patrick wasn't much interested in school or work. It seemed to people who knew him that Patrick had no useful talents except one: he "could send his voice out so that it could be heard clearly at a distance." Patrick's Uncle Langloo also had such a "sending voice"; when he gave a political speech, he could make people's hair stand on end. No one would have guessed that one day Patrick Henry's voice would do even more.

On May 29th, 1752, Patrick Henry became sixteen. He was six feet tall, a lanky, sharp-boned young man with flashing blue eyes, generally dressed in checked breeches and a jumpshirt, generally in his bare feet. He was old enough now to be counted among the men in Virginia and old enough to make his own living. And where was he?

Well, he may have been stretched out on a sack of salt. People claimed this was Patrick's favorite resting place and he rested a good deal. His father

Brief marginal notes provide pronunciations and definitions of words and clarify and highlight portions of the text.

Lesson continued on next page. ▶

Discussion Questions encourage students to interpret and apply what they have read.

Optional group and individual activities encourage a wide range of student response through composition, oral interpretation, dramatization, art, and other forms of expression.

Discussion Questions *A biography is the story of a person's life. Why is this story called a* historical biography? (Because the story is about the life of Patrick Henry, a person who played a part in American history.) *What lesson can be learned from Patrick Henry's life?* (Despite difficulty, a person must keep trying to succeed.)
Enriching Activities 1. *News headlines/ stories.* Have the students write newspaper headlines and short articles about important events in Patrick Henry's life. **2.** *Speech writing.* Ask the students to write speeches on issues they feel strongly about. Suggest that they make outlines before writing and rehearse their speeches before presenting them to the class. **3.** *Costume fair.* Ask students to dress as the American hero of their choice. Organize a Great Americans Day parade, ask for brief reports about each character, and have an old-fashioned American picnic lunch.

Questions

1. At the trial of his first big case, Patrick Henry wished two people would *not* be there. Who were these two people? Tell why one of these people went home and why one stayed.

2. Patrick Henry became a great speaker, or *orator*. How did people react when they first heard his speeches? What did his speeches persuade the people of the colonies to do?

3. Why did the crowd become so excited when Patrick Henry cried, ''Give me liberty or give me death''?

4. Match these words with their definitions.
(page 364) client   a. obeyed
(page 367) attorney   b. revoked
(page 368) complied   c. lawyer
(page 372) repealed   d. customer

Literal/recall *Making time lines.* The students may list any of the dates and events given below:

Activity

The biography of Patrick Henry begins on May 29, 1752. It closes on May 29, 1777. Draw a long line with one of those dates at each end. Find five very important happenings in Patrick Henry's life between those two dates. Write them on the time line you have drawn to show when they happened.

1754—marries Sarah Shelton; 1757—gives up farming; 1761— becomes a lawyer; 1763—wins the Parsons' Case; 1765—member of the House of Burgesses; 1773—speech against tea tax; 1775—''Give me liberty'' speech.

Answers to the questions in the student's book are given on the same page as the student questions. Page numbers provide references for re-reading.

1. Literal/recall His uncle and his father. Patrick asked his uncle to go home and he complied. Patrick's father was the presiding judge so he could not leave. (pages 368–369)
2. Literal/recall and **Interpretive/ inference** At first, the people were wild with excitement. Later, Henry's speeches persuaded the jury in the Parsons' Case to give the parsons less restitution; his resolutions against taxation encouraged colonists to oppose taxation; his liberty speech persuaded people to fight for independence. (pages 371–376)
3. Literal/recall and **Interpretive/ inference** Possible answer: the crowd was upset about the issue and inspired by Patrick Henry's words. (page 376)
4. Vocabulary client—d.; attorney—c.; complied—b.; repealed—a.

Each question is identified by two labels (e.g., literal/ recall). The first label refers to the type of reading skill students must use to answer the question. The second label identifies the type of question being asked.

377

A special guide for the teacher

"Teaching Literature in the Classroom" is a special guide for the teacher who wants to enrich and extend students' reading of literature. It includes suggestions for such activities as dramatization, writing, language, and art projects.

From Levels 1-8 Teacher's Editions

Teaching Literature in the Classroom *Sam Leaton Sebesta*

I hear, and I forget.
I see, and I remember.
I do, and I understand.

Chinese proverb

A S TEACHERS, we want children and young people to discover the joy of reading literature. With this discovery, they become free to pursue this pleasure independently, now and throughout their lifetimes. But we want something more for the young people we teach. We want them to be able to read literature not only with pleasure, but also with understanding. We want them to be able to respond thoughtfully to their reading—to *interact* with it—so that both their pleasure and their knowledge are increased.

Students' interaction with literature begins with teachers who approach literature with joy and excitement. Once a teacher shares this enthusiasm with students, the stage is set for their own interaction with literature, which can be as multifaceted as the teacher and the students wish to make it. This interaction can also be fostered by a good literature program that offers teachers both depth and breadth of selection, as well as providing a structure for helping students to understand and appreciate literature.

Good literary instruction proceeds in a two-phase cycle. First, reading a good selection motivates students to respond expressively to what they have read. Second, proper guidance of their responses enables

students to build knowledge and skills that help them understand the next selection they encounter. The goal of such a process is students' continued reading and increasing enjoyment of literature.

The following discussion will provide a number of general guidelines as well as practical ideas for using literature in the classroom. The ideas are divided into four sections, beginning with the reading experience and discussion of literature and then considering other responses to literature—oral and written composition, interpretive reading and dramatization, and the arts. Methodological questions are raised and answered as each section and its activities are developed. Many suggestions for activities are also included throughout the lessons in this Teacher's Edition.

The Reading Experience

PREPARING FOR READING

For beginning readers, the first reading of a poem or a story is a shared experience, with the teacher reading aloud and the students joining in on a refrain or a predictable passage. Beyond this stage, students can be expected to read selections independently, but guidance and motivation are still important. The Teacher's Editions for this program offer suggestions for such guided preparation for reading: questions to raise

T30

Introduction to ODYSSEY

Tell me, Muse, of the man of many ways, who was driven
far journeys, after he had sacked Troy's sacred citadel.
Many were they whose cities he saw, whose minds he learned of,
many the pains he suffered in his spirit on the wide sea,
struggling for his own life and the homecoming of his companions.
. . . .
. . . Goddess, daughter of Zeus, speak, and begin our story.

The Odyssey of Homer

THE "MAN OF MANY WAYS" was
Odysseus—king of Ithaca in ancient
Greece, hero in the war against
Troy, husband of Penelope, father of Tele-
machus, and, in all his endeavors, a man of
unusual cunning and courage. Homer's
great epic poem the *Odyssey* recounts
Odysseus' long wandering journey home
from the Trojan War. Three thousand years
later, the *Odyssey* remains one of the
enduring works of literature, and Odysseus,
one of the enduring heroes.

When we hear the word *odyssey* today,
we think of more than the epic journey of
Odysseus. For as the word has become
part of our language, it has taken on other
meanings: a long wandering, a series of
adventurous journeys marked by many
changes of fortune, an intellectual or spiri-
tual quest. In its broadest sense, we could
say that odyssey describes the lifelong
journey that all people undertake from birth.

It is that continuing human odyssey and
our continuing wonder about it that are at
the center of all literature. Though it is
history that records our deeds, it is literature
that seeks to express our thoughts, feelings,
dreams, and wonderings about the world.

Since its origins in the chants and tales of
unknown storytellers, literature has recorded
events vividly, recalled our shared experience, and taught us about ourselves. In
doing so, it has come to us in diverse
forms—both oral and written—and in divergent voices, the sum of which is our literary
heritage, drawn from the past and growing
into the future.

Children's literature is one part of our
literary heritage that has experienced
remarkable growth in this century. With
more than forty thousand children's books
in print, the range of genres and content
available to young people today is far
greater than ever before.

While there is no lack of literature for
children, however, the problem of selecting reading can be a difficult one. Some
literary works meet children's interests
better than others do. There are books that
may be more suitable for children at a particular developmental stage or that may
offer greater aesthetic growth because of
their style, content, or theme. Young people
need help in selecting literature that offers
the best foundation both for their reading
pleasure now, and for a lifetime.

In many instances, that foundation is begun at home, when parents read aloud to their children, share books with them, and talk with them about what they have read. In others, it may begin at school, when teachers and librarians read to students, encourage them to read independently, and support their spontaneous responses to reading. To a large extent, basal reading programs build on that foundation by providing a range of literature for learning and enjoyment throughout the grade levels.

In basal reading programs, however, the literature strand is only one strand in many, and the development of such basic reading skills as decoding and comprehension usually takes precedence over skills of literary appreciation and understanding. In addition, literature is often used as a vehicle to teach skills in the language arts or to enrich and extend other content areas. Despite our best efforts to provide students with a "basic education," we have often forgotten that literature is a basic subject that deserves its own place in the elementary school curriculum.

Purposes of ODYSSEY

ODYSSEY is a carefully planned program designed to provide children with a basic literary education. The program's selections and instructional material are all aimed toward its main objective: to provide a solid foundation of literary experiences on which students may build a lifetime of reading pleasure. To reach this objective, ODYSSEY has the following goals:

- To offer students a wide variety of pleasurable, independent reading of the highest literary quality
- To demonstrate the value of literature and to foster interest in reading

- To increase understanding of literature's relationship to human experience
- To develop insights into personal thoughts, feelings, and experiences
- To promote recognition of the individual's role in the community and society
- To develop an awareness of other people and cultures
- To show the power and possibilities of language as a tool for self-expression and to develop an awareness of the persuasive or manipulatory power of words
- To develop an understanding of literary forms, techniques, and styles
- To demonstrate the unique artistry of individual authors and illustrators
- To encourage thoughtful and critical responses to literature and to develop respect for the responses of others
- To develop the skills of reading comprehension, writing, and the other language arts, as well as logical thinking skills

Criteria for Selections

In choosing selections for ODYSSEY, the program's developers consulted children's literature specialists, teachers, librarians— and children and young people themselves. After potential selections were identified, program consultants (see pages T4 and T5) evaluated each selection using the following criteria:

Interest Level.   Is the selection likely to interest children at this age level?

Reading Level.   Will most of the children at this level be able to read the selection independently?

Quality.   Does the selection have high literary quality?

Experience. Is the selection worthwhile, either because it brings pure enjoyment to young readers or because it fosters their personal growth?

Portrayal of Ethnic, Minority, and Special Groups. Does the selection portray all groups fairly?

Further considerations were the selections' relevance to six thematic strands and their balance in such areas as content, literary type, multicultural representation, and authorship. The final choices were made after extensive classroom testing.

Organization of ODYSSEY

The literature in ODYSSEY is organized thematically around six strands. Beginning with Reader One, the strands form the basis of six thematic units in each textbook.

STRANDS IN ODYSSEY

GROWING AND CHANGING	Roles, relationships, and personal growth
ADVENTURE AND SUSPENSE	Real and imaginary adventures
HUMOR	The humorous side of life
FANTASY	Realms of the imagination
EARTH, SEA, AND SPACE	Humans and the natural world
QUEST AND HEROISM	The many aspects of courage

The thematic strands in the program appear in the chart on pages T24 and T25.

Readability in ODYSSEY

In ODYSSEY, prose selections below grade level are usually labeled *Easy,* selections at grade level are labeled *Average,* and selections above grade level are labeled *Challenging.* The selections were evaluated on the basis of their syntactic and conceptual difficulty as well as by the appropriate readability formula.

Level One. Because most first-grade children are not independent readers, the selections in the three textbooks at Level One are intended for teacher-directed reading and for shared reading experiences. For example, the teacher might begin by reading aloud a selection such as a poem with a refrain or a story with repetition or predictable ''next sentences.'' The teacher can then invite the class to ''take the next part'' or to read aloud in unison. Simple plays—usually presented in the Readers Theatre format—provide still more opportunities for shared reading experiences. To promote oral language development, the Level One readers include content-rich pictures and wordless picture stories so that children may tell or write the story they ''read'' in the illustrations. Some easy stories, which are labeled as such in the Teacher's Editions, can be read independently by able readers.

Levels Two through Eight. At Levels Two and Three, most prose selections meet the reading abilities of average and above-average readers, with the majority of the selections falling within the average range, as determined mainly by the Spache readability formula. At Levels Four through Eight, most selections continue to meet the reading abilities of the average reader, with the range of reading levels widening to include more selections for below-average and gifted readers. Readability of Levels Four through Eight has been determined mainly by the Dale-Chall readability formula. Since the Dale-Chall readability level of much adult literature is seventh- to eighth-grade, however, in Levels Seven and Eight the label *Challenging* means at or above seventh-grade level; *Average,* sixth grade; *Easy,* fifth grade and below.

Evaluation in the Program

In evaluating the program's success in the classroom, the central question should be whether the selections have enhanced the students' enjoyment of literature. This is an affective outcome that no written test can assess, but teachers can assess progress informally, asking students for their opinions about the literature; listening to their spontaneous comments, especially their expressions of interest in reading and literature; and observing whether they seek out further literary experiences. Brief anecdotal records of the students' responses will provide valid and direct evidence that the program's goal is being met.

The questions and activities in the program can be used to evaluate the students' knowledge of literary elements and techniques, and their growth in literary appreciation, reading comprehension, and both oral and written composition. Questions at the literal level will yield brief yet adequate information on students' abilities in literal comprehension. Questions at the interpretive level can provide information about students' abilities to make inferences, to express opinions based on their reading, and to substantiate both kinds of responses. Questions that require critical thinking skills can assess students' abilities to read ''beyond the lines,'' that is, to integrate

what they have read with their own experience or to apply it in a different context. Even though their answers to critical-level questions are subjective and thus will vary greatly, the students' responses can be evaluated in terms of their fluency, flexibility, elaboration, originality, and logic.

Literature for a Lifetime

A literature program for children requires faith in the lasting effects of teaching and learning. Such faith seems warranted. Most adults who like to read literature can describe one or a hundred rewarding contacts with books in childhood and adolescence. Many such readers might identify with Francie, the child in Betty Smith's novel *A Tree Grows in Brooklyn,* who realizes suddenly the benefits of having learned to read:

> From that time on, the world was hers for the reading. She would never be lonely again, never miss the lack of intimate friends. Books became her friends and there was one for every mood. There was poetry for quiet companionship. There was adventure when she tired of quiet hours. There would be love stories when she came into adolescence and when she wanted to feel a closeness to someone she could read a biography. On that day when she first knew she could read, she made a vow to read one book a day as long as she lived.

The journeys children take through books can carry them as near as a city street or as far away as a dragon's lair; but wherever their reading leads them, the discovery of literature in childhood can extend and enrich their lives far beyond that time. In books readers may live more lives, try on more costumes, step into more situations than any one life could possibly afford. ODYSSEY is just the beginning of that life-long journey through literature.

Thematic Strands in ODYSSEY

Level	GROWING AND CHANGING	ADVENTURE AND SUSPENSE	HUMOR
1★	**Let's Go Together** Relationships with friends and family	**Far, Far Away** The call of adventure	**What a Surprise!** Humorous experiences with an element of surprise
2	**We Could Be Friends** The many aspects of friendship	**Something Is There** Mysterious happenings	**Tell Me Something Very Silly** Comical characters; improbable occurrences
3	**Good Times** Building relationships	**You Can't Catch Me** Ingenious escapes from danger	**It's Not Funny** Humorous predicaments
4	**When Paths Cross** Contrasting points of view	**Across the Land and Sea** Journeys to new lands	**What a Character!** Remarkable characters in humorous situations
5	**Never Give Up** The role of perseverance in personal growth	**Facing the Unknown** Suspenseful encounters in different settings	**It Must Be a Trick** Tricksters and trickery
6	**Dream Keepers** Recognizing individual identity and talents	**Expect the Unexpected** Unexpected encounters and surprise endings	**Funny Side Up** Mix-ups, mishaps, and misunderstandings
7	**Reflections** Experiences leading to personal growth and life changes	**On a Moonless Night** Strange occurrences	**Monkey Business** The techniques of humor
8	**Spectrum** The many paths to self-knowledge and maturity	**Only Darkness Ticking** The techniques of suspense	**On the Funny Side** Humor in ordinary and extraordinary situations

★Refers only to Level 1 Reader. Strands are not grouped by units in Preprimer and Primer.

FANTASY	EARTH, SEA, AND SPACE	QUEST AND HEROISM
Tell Me a Story Adventures of fantasy characters	***I Wonder*** The wonders of nature	***I'm Growing*** Awareness of physical growth
Long, Long Ago Magical beings, places, and things	***Animals All Around*** Animals and their environments	***I Can Do It!*** Acting independently and assuming new roles
Would You Believe It! Tall tales	***There Is a Season . . .*** The cycle of the seasons	***Tell Me the Name*** Awareness of personal identity
When the Moon Shines Illusions and transformations	***To Live with Animals*** Relationships between animals and humans	***Problems and Puzzles*** Meeting challenges and solving problems
Truly Amazing Talents Characters with amazing or unusual talents	***To Live with Nature*** Living with the creatures and forces of nature; survival	***From America's Past*** Characters and events from American history
Time Travelers Exploring time through fantasy	***A Tree of Ice,*** ***A Rain of Stars*** Nature as a source of inspiration and beliefs	***Tests of Courage*** The many forms of courage in myth, legend, and contemporary life
A Gift of Story Greek myths and epic heroes	***Voices from the Earth*** Encounters with animals and elements in nature	***To Stand Alone*** Individual courage in the face of adversity
Another Where, ***Another When*** The elements and varieties of fantasy	***Secrets*** The interrelationship of humans and nature	***We, the People*** The importance of ordinary people in American history

Skills Index for Level Five

This Skills Index will help you to locate the pages on which each listed skill is presented in a level of ODYSSEY: AN HBJ LITERATURE PROGRAM. Boldfaced page references indicate that the skill is presented in the pupil's textbook. Other references are to teaching suggestions and activities in the Teacher's Edition.

   The numbers preceding the items in the index correspond to the HBJ Skills Code. This code may be used to correlate skills in ODYSSEY with other language arts and reading programs published after 1980 by Harcourt Brace Jovanovich. Teachers who wish to cross-reference these programs may do so by referring to these same numbers that appear in other programs. The index can also serve as a basis for correlating ODYSSEY with the management system or curriculum guide used in your school.

Skills Code Number	SKILL	PAGES
	COMPREHENSION	
3.1	**To Recognize Concepts**	
3.1.4	to relate reading to experience	16, **30**, 38, 48, 70, **113**, 172, 175, 193, 206, 234, 237, **254**, 275, 277, **308**, 308, 313, **325**, 327, 343, **358**
3.2	**To Classify**	
3.2.1	to classify by common attributes or association	76, 77, 256–257
3.3	**To Identify and Use Literal Comprehension Skills**	
3.3.1	to find or recall specific details	**30**, 39, **95**, 97, **113**, 113, 131, **146**, 146, **171**, 175, **205**, 217, 233, **254, 275, 292, 308, 325, 340**, 340, **358, 377**, 387
3.3.3	to identify stated cause and effect relationships	**95, 191, 275, 292, 358, 377**, 405
3.3.6.1	to understand the meaning of phrases and/or sentences	**30**, 138, **275, 325, 402**
3.3.6.2	to relate word order to sentence meaning	218
3.3.6.4	to recognize the same idea stated in different words or to state information in different words	**30**, 36, 172, **191**, 212, 217, 294, **308, 325**
3.3.7.1	to recognize or interpret time order and time relationships	172, 308, 310, **377**

Skills Code Number	SKILL	PAGES
3.3.7.4	to recognize sequence of events	**171, 233, 254,** 308
3.3.7.5	to identify stages or events in a selection	**30, 171,** 275
3.3.8.5	to identify comparison and contrast	212, 311
3.4	**To Make Inferences**	
3.4.1	to draw conclusions	30, 72, **233,** 275, 309, 343, **402**
3.4.2	to predict outcomes	21, 70, 275
3.4.3	to make generalizations	377
3.4.4	to make judgments	**131,** 131, **325, 358**
3.4.5	to distinguish between reality and fantasy	39, **113**
3.4.6	to recognize, make, or complete an analogy	292
3.4.7	to recognize the unstated main idea	212, 292, 342
3.4.8	to identify unstated cause and effect relationships	30, **113,** 131, 146, **191, 205,** 205, **254,** 254, 292, **325,** 340
3.5	**To Identify and Use Word Meanings**	**64–65,** 65, **66,** 66, **95, 113, 131,** 131, **146, 205, 254, 292, 358**
3.5.1	to identify and use homophones	**64–65,** 65, **66,** 66
3.5.5	to identify and use multiple meanings of words	**64–65,** 65, **66,** 66
3.6	**To Identify and Use Critical and Judgmental Reading Skills**	
3.6.7	to distinguish between facts and fictional details	**377, 378–385,** 402
3.6.8	to identify information on which stated conclusions are based	48
3.7	**To Relate Reading to Illustrations**	119, 247, **378–379, 380**
3.8	**To Extrapolate from, or Extend, a Literary Work**	**95, 131, 146, 191,** 217, **233,** 275, 292, 340, 358, 402
	APPRECIATION	
6.1	**To Develop Oral Reading and Choral Speaking Skills**	113, 257, 310, 311
6.2	**To Recognize Forms of Writing: Poetry**	**14–15, 32–37, 70–71, 72–73, 74–77, 96–97, 172–173, 206, 212, 216–217, 234, 256–257, 294, 309, 310, 311, 342, 386–387, 411**
6.2.1	to recognize humorous poetry	**14–15, 32–37,** 36, **70–71, 72–73, 96–97, 216–217, 256–257**
6.2.8	to recognize free verse	**342,** 342
6.3	**To Recognize Forms of Writing: Plays**	**48–63**

Skills Code Number	SKILL	PAGES
6.4	**To Recognize Forms of Writing: Fiction**	
6.4.3.1	to recognize folk tales	**218–232**
6.4.3.3	to recognize songs and ballads	**406–407, 408–410**
6.4.3.4	to recognize riddles	**64–65, 66, 309**
6.4.4	to recognize myths	**132–145**
6.4.5	to recognize stories	**16–29, 38–47, 78–94, 110–112, 114–130, 150–170, 174–190, 192–204, 236–253, 276–291, 299–307, 326–339, 344–357**
6.4.7	to recognize historical fiction	**388–401,** 402
6.4.8	to recognize science fiction	**312–324**
6.4.10	to recognize fantasy	**258–274**
6.5	**To Recognize Forms of Writing: Nonfiction**	**98–99,** 99, **404–405,** 404–405
6.5.1	to recognize biography	**362–376,** 377, **378–385,** 379, 380, 385
6.5.2	to recognize autobiography	308
6.6	**To Identify Elements of Poetry: To Recognize Aspects of Style**	
6.6.1	to identify rhyme	**74–77,** 75, 76, 77
6.6.2.2	to identify the quatrain	**74–77,** 75, 76, 77
6.6.3	to recognize rhythm and meter	74, **77,** 77
6.6.4	to interpret mood	343
6.6.5	to recognize humor	39, **64–65**
6.6.6.2	to recognize alliteration	15
6.6.6.3	to recognize sensory imagery	282, 405
6.6.6.4	to recognize simile	**402**
6.6.6.5	to recognize metaphor	**212,** 212, 309, 311
6.6.6.7	to recognize word play	35, **64–65, 66, 96–97,** 257
6.6.6.8	to recognize personification	309, 311
6.6.6.9	to recognize repetition	**233,** 233, 386, 409, 411
6.6.6.10	to distinguish between literal and figurative language	411
6.6.7	to identify the speaker's voice in poetry	206, 406
6.8	**To Compare and Contrast Selections**	**309–311,** 311
6.9	**To Identify Characterization**	
6.9.1	to identify major and minor characters	**171**
6.9.2	to compare and contrast characters	113, 292, 358
6.9.3	to recognize an author's techniques of characterization	**208–211**
6.9.3.1	to recognize characterization through an author's description of a character	**209, 210–211**

Skills Code Number	SKILL	PAGES
6.9.3.3	to recognize characterization through characters' words and actions	**208, 210–211, 275, 308,** 325
6.9.4	to interpret characters' feelings and traits in literature	30, **95, 113,** 131, **171,** 171, **205,** 206, **340**
6.10	**To Identify Setting**	
6.10.1	to identify elements of setting	**131,** 275, **340, 402**
6.10.3	to recognize the relationship between setting and other story elements	308, 325
6.11	**To Identify Plot**	406
6.11.1.1	to recognize problem	**191, 275,** 325, 340
6.11.1.3	to recognize solution	**191, 275,** 325
6.14	**To Recognize the Relationship Between an Author's Life and Work**	**31, 207, 235, 255, 293, 341, 403**
6.15	**To Recognize Satire or Irony**	
6.15.1	to recognize verbal irony	120
6.17	**To Appreciate the Origins of Literature**	
6.17.1	to appreciate the languages and/or literatures of different cultures	**32–37, 38–47, 78–94, 114–130, 132–145, 192–204, 218–232, 234–235, 310, 311, 326–339, 342, 404–405, 411**
6.17.2	to identify the historical/cultural background of a literary work	32, 33, 115, 133, 151, 234, 310, 363, 389, **408**
6.17.3	to understand the oral tradition	234
	COMPOSITION: ORAL AND WRITTEN	
7.1	**To Write Functionally**	
7.1.1	to write a complete sentence	**275**
7.1.2	to write a paragraph	71, **95,** 95, **171,** 191, **205, 211,** 211, **233, 254,** 294, 402
7.1.2.2	to write a descriptive paragraph	**211,** 211
7.1.3	to write a list	65, **211,** 308, **358,** 358
7.1.4	to write directions	205, **358**
7.1.5	to write an outline	377
7.1.7	to write a letter	**113, 191,** 191
7.1.8	to write a diary entry	**30,** 233
7.1.10	to take written notes	**308**
7.1.14	to write an article	99, **254,** 377, 402
7.1.15.1	to write interview questions	171, 385
7.1.17	to write a report	**325,** 377

Skills Code Number	SKILL	PAGES
7.2	**To Write Creatively**	
7.2.3	to write using special devices and conventions	66
7.2.3.2	to write a metaphor	212, 309
7.2.3.5	to write an example of personification	309
7.2.4	to write a story	**131, 292**
7.2.5.3	to write a legend	146
7.2.6	to write a poem	77, 340, 342, 343
7.2.7.2	to write dialogue	206, **380,** 385
7.2.8	to write a speech	377, 405
7.2.9.1	to write a biography	**380, 384–385,** 385, 387

Activities Index

Oral Language and Listening

Classifying	77
Creating a game	254
Developing discussion skills	15, 30, 36, 48, 71, 76, 95, 113, 131, 146, 171, 173, 191, 205, 206, 211, 217, 233, 234, 254, 275, 292, 294, 308, 325, 340, 342, 343, 358, 377, 380, 402, 406
Giving an oral report	377, 411
Making a speech	377, 405
Oral reading	257, 310, 311
Storytelling	**233,** 233

Vocabulary Development — **64–65,** 65, **66,** 66, **113,** 131

Composition: Oral and Written

Composing poetry	77, 257, 340, 342, 343
Creating figures of speech	212, 309
Doing research	99, 145, 191, 308, 411
Writing biographies	**380, 386**
Writing dialogues	266, **380**
Writing diary entries	30, 233
Writing directions	205, **358**
Writing heroic tales	146
Writing interview questions	171
Writing letters	**113, 191,** 191
Writing lists	65, **211,** 308 **358,** 358
Writing newspaper articles	99, **254,** 377, 402
Writing newspaper headlines	377
Writing notes	**308**

Writing outlines   377
Writing puns   66
Writing reports   **325,** 377, 411
Writing speeches   377, 405
Writing sentences and paragraphs   71, **95,** 95, **171,** 191, **205, 211,** 211, **233,** 294, 402
Writing stories   **131, 292**
Writing tongue twisters   15

Drama

Improvisation   37, 95, 171, **205,** 275, 292, 402
Pantomime   37
Play production   49, 254, 325
Puppetry   37, 65
Readers Theatre   113
Story Theater   39

Art

Drawing or painting   73, 97, **146,** 173, 191, **205,** 217, 292, 294, 311, 325, **402,** 405, 406
Making books   311
Making collages   30
Making maps   275, **340**
Making models   71
Making time lines   308, **377**

Other Activities

Learning about animals (science)   191, 308
Making time lines (social studies)   308, 377
Related reading (language arts)   **67,** 73, 97, **147, 207, 213, 255,** 274, **295,** 340, **341, 359, 403,** 410, **412**
Singing/Music (humanities)   311, **408,** 410
Staging a costume fair (social studies)   377
Using maps (social studies)   275, **340,** 389

Teaching Literature in the Classroom
Sam Leaton Sebesta

I hear, and I forget.
I see, and I remember.
I do, and I understand.

Chinese proverb

A S TEACHERS, we want children and young people to discover the joy of reading literature. With this discovery, they become free to pursue this pleasure independently, now and throughout their lifetimes. But we want something more for the young people we teach. We want them to be able to read literature not only with pleasure, but also with understanding. We want them to be able to respond thoughtfully to their reading—to *interact* with it—so that both their pleasure and their knowledge are increased.

Students' interaction with literature begins with teachers who approach literature with joy and excitement. Once a teacher shares this enthusiasm with students, the stage is set for their own interaction with literature, which can be as multifaceted as the teacher and the students wish to make it. This interaction can also be fostered by a good literature program that offers teachers both depth and breadth of selection, as well as providing a structure for helping students to understand and appreciate literature.

Good literary instruction proceeds in a two-phase cycle. First, reading a good selection motivates students to respond expressively to what they have read. Second, proper guidance of their responses enables students to build knowledge and skills that help them understand the next selection they encounter. The goal of such a process is students' continued reading and increasing enjoyment of literature.

The following discussion will provide a number of general guidelines as well as practical ideas for using literature in the classroom. The ideas are divided into four sections, beginning with the reading experience and discussion of literature and then considering other responses to literature—oral and written composition, interpretive reading and dramatization, and the arts. Methodological questions are raised and answered as each section and its activities are developed. Many suggestions for activities are also included throughout the lessons in this Teacher's Edition.

The Reading Experience

PREPARING FOR READING

For beginning readers, the first reading of a poem or a story is a shared experience, with the teacher reading aloud and the students joining in on a refrain or a predictable passage. Beyond this stage, students can be expected to read selections independently, but guidance and motivation are still important. The Teacher's Editions for this program offer suggestions for such guided preparation for reading: questions to raise before the reading takes place; brief comments about the work that is to be read; and *definitions* of key terms to help students understand the selection.

Preparation may require only a few moments, but it is useful for several reasons. It allows students to begin reading with a "warmed-up motor," prepared to respond to the selection. It helps students establish a focus for reading. And it helps remove the barriers that unfamiliar words may otherwise present. Research has shown that preteaching relevant vocabulary increases student comprehension.

SILENT AND ORAL READING

Most reading specialists recommend that first readings always be silent, independent readings. They point out that silent reading permits each student to read at his or her own pace. It also encourages reflection and allows both time for response and the chance to go back and *reread* a passage before going on. Initial silent reading helps students enjoy and interpret a selection further during a later oral reading.

This recommendation for silent reading first has exceptions. Most poems should be read aloud initially. Anecdotes and funny stories beg for sharing and may lose their appeal if assigned to be read silently. When the language or theme of a selection is complex, guided oral reading helps students share the literary experience from the start.

At no time, however, should oral reading be considered a mere exercise in "getting all the words right." Rather, it is a means to guiding understanding. Most often, this guidance is better done by (1) *preparing students to read silently*, (2) *encouraging silent reading according to each student's rate and reading strategies*, and (3) *later having students reread all or part of a*

selection for a purpose—to support a point, to share an enthusiasm, or to enliven a work through oral interpretation.

DISCUSSING A SELECTION

Once a selection is read, discussion can enhance the literary experience. The main purpose of such discussion is to allow students to speak, to express their responses to the literature they are reading, and to listen to the varied responses of their classmates. In addition, discussion can be an informal way for you to assess students' enjoyment, involvement, and understanding of what they have read. Asking a general opening question and inviting students to ask questions are good ways to begin a discussion that leads to more structured questions and activities.

Opening discussion should be non-threatening. It should invite immediate, pertinent response. It should, if possible, set the stage for more focused questions and activities. Here are three effective ways to begin a discussion. (Consult each selection in the Teacher's Edition for specific suggestions.)

1. *Ask what students discovered as a result of their reading.* Sometimes this may be a focusing question, based on a preparation question posed before the reading. Sometimes the question can be a more general opener—"Tell me about the story"—that invites students to share their responses, fresh from reading, without imposing a structure.

2. *Refer to the question-and-activity page in the pupil's textbook*, which is included after most of the longer prose selections. Students who have prepared responses to items on the page will have something to contribute at once, and discussion will get off to a good start.

3. *Ask each student to find one passage in the story that is exciting to read aloud—a segment that might entice a listener to read the entire story.* Subsequent discussion can begin with a request for justification: "Why did you choose that part?"

Early in the discussion, invite student questions: "What did you wonder about as you read the story? Did a question come to your mind as you read this poem?" Such a procedure encourages self-generated questioning as one reads, a basic strategy that good readers use constantly.

Inquiry Within the Program. In ODYSSEY, a variety of questions help teachers focus and extend discussions about literature, and also help provide well-rounded, unified lessons. Some of the questions are derived from objectives stated in the teaching notes preceding each selection. Others review objectives from earlier readings or seek to broaden the lesson. In each case, questions pertain to the central meaning and significance of the work, their chief purpose being to enhance students' enjoyment and understanding and to allow them to use their listening, speaking, and writing skills when responding.

The following are the five types of questions used in the ODYSSEY program:

1. **Recall** *questions ask the student to specify information, or data, present in the story, poem, or nonfiction selection.* Students are not asked to recall random facts, but information derived from the focus of the selection. Often this information is used in subsequent higher-level discussion. With some students, the recall level needs little attention. With others, you may need to elicit additional recall, such as sequence of events, before proceeding to discuss a selection above the literal level.

2. **Inference** *questions are based on the information given in a selection, but they require more than simple recall.* Inference questions require conjectures from the student based on knowledge of the selection's content, on personal experience, and on imagination. The author of a story, for example, may present three details, three "facts" about the setting from which the reader is expected to infer additional details. Many readers do this automatically, but some do not. Inference questions, then, give practice and encouragement in figuring out what happened between events described in a story, in determining whose point of view is presented in a poem, or in speculating about cause and effect when the relationship is implied rather than directly described. This type of question recognizes that no literary work *tells* all. Rather, every literary work *suggests*, and the reader interacts by inferring the missing parts. Much of the fun of reading literature comes from inference.

3. **Extrapolation** *questions, extensions of inference, invite the reader to consider, for example, what happened after the story ended, how a character might act in another situation, or what the speaker of a poem might say about an object or scene other than that described in the poem.* (*To extrapolate* means "to project, extend or expand something that is known into an unknown area; to conjecture.") Extrapolation questions are often more extensive and more speculative than inference questions, and they may extend creative thinking toward writing, drawing, or speaking.[1]

4. **Relating reading to experience** *questions, as the term is used here, are those questions that invite the reader to relate the literary work directly to his or her own life.* The basic form for this question is "How is your own experience *like* some-

---

1. Robert A. Collins, "Extrapolation: Going Beyond the Present," *Media and Methods*, 16, no. 3 (November 1979); 22–25.

thing in the selection you have just read?"
A variation is "Based on your experience,
what would you have done in the situation
described in this selection?" Throughout
the program, this basic idea is varied to
meet the specifics of a story, a poem, or a
work of nonfiction.

5. **Language and vocabulary** *questions are closed-answer items to check a
reader's knowledge of key terms, idioms, or
stylistic features.* A part of literary awareness resides in understanding what words
mean as well as in understanding nuances
of style.

As explained on page T18 of this textbook, each question and activity in the
ODYSSEY program also has a label identifying the reading skill students will use
when responding. These skills are **literal**,
interpretive, and **critical thinking**.

Using Questions to Teach.   The question types described above are used in
ODYSSEY mainly for teaching purposes,
not testing. Most questions can start a
series of responses, and one question may
lead to another without interrupting the
main topic of discussion. The resulting
pattern of discussion may not be question–
answer, question–answer, as it is likely to
be in testing. Instead, the pattern for the
discussion of a story may be the following:
a question asking for clarification of a word
or phrase leads to a question involving
recall of the story events, which in turn
leads to a question asking for an interpretation of a character's reaction to those
events.

Try applying some of the following strategies during your classroom discussions:

1. *Probing.* A probe can be a request for
additional information to clarify or elaborate
on a response, or it can be a request for
other answers. Such questions as "Any
other ideas?" or "Can you tell us *more*

about that idea?" can develop a discussion
without fragmenting it. Listen to a response
and decide whether a probe is needed.

2. *Requesting verification.* Ask students
to return to the text in order to verify a point.
Students may be asked to substantiate
opinions as well as locate bases for statements of fact. At other times students
may be called upon to use other sources,
including their own experience, to verify a
statement.

3. *Providing wait time.* The *wait time*, or
think time, principle simply means that a
time of silence comes between a question
and a response.[2] Research shows that
classes using wait time have better discussions. Responses are longer, and students
show higher-level thinking than when the
wait time principle is ignored.

To apply this strategy, you might begin
by saying, "Now I'm going to ask you a
very thought-provoking question. Take time
to think about it before you tell us what you
think." Ask the question, and then allow
several seconds to elapse before calling for
a response. *After* hearing a response, wait
several seconds before commenting or
asking for other responses.

EVALUATING READING EXPERIENCES

To evaluate whether your literature discussions, along with pre-reading preparation
and silent, independent reading, are of benefit to the students, observe students on the
following:

1. *Notice whether students seem to seek
new reading experiences and whether literature lessons are eagerly anticipated.* If

---

2. Linda B. Gambrell, "Think-Time: Implications for
Reading Instruction," *The Reading Teacher*, 34, no. 2
(November 1980); 143–146.

these reactions occur, the students are attaining the goals of the reading experience, including pleasure, insight into human behavior, and appreciation for language and style.

2. *Consider students' responses during discussions*. Do they enter discussions enthusiastically? Do all contribute? Is there a give-and-take during the discussions that seems to produce a deepened understanding of the selection? (The importance of building enthusiasm should not be underestimated. Each new reading experience enjoyed by a child makes it less likely that he or she will become a nonreader.)

3. *Consider students' answers to the questions themselves, in order to identify their level of reading comprehension*. The literal level items (recall, vocabulary) are usually easy to evaluate since they call for *convergent* thinking. This means that students will come to an agreement on a "right answer." Though suggested "right answers" are provided in the Teacher's Edition, students' answers may vary and still be "right."

Above-literal items (inference, extrapolation, relating reading to experience) seek to develop *divergent* thinking. This means that students' answers will be different from one another since they are based on individual opinion and experience. Although examples of responses are presented in the Teacher's Editions and labeled "Possible answer(s)," no one can predict the range of responses that can arise from divergent thinking. The following criteria can be used, however, in evaluating such responses:

- *Fluency*. Do students contribute easily to the discussion? Are they able to produce many responses?
- *Flexibility*. Are responses varied so that several *different* ideas are contributed?
- *Originality*. Are some students' responses creative as well as appropriate to

the question; that is, do some students demonstrate a unique ability to discern and to solve the problems posed by the question?
- *Elaboration*. When probed, can students expand their responses by adding details?

4. *Observe the students' responses to the reading through activities such as oral or written composition, dramatization, or creative expression in the arts*. If the reading experience and discussion are indeed promoting students' responses to literature, activities will help reveal and develop such responses.

Additional Readings

Torrance, E. Paul, and Myers, R. E., *Creative Learning and Teaching.* New York: Dodd, Mead, 1970. Chapters 7 through 10 contain suggestions for asking good divergent-thinking questions, with factors to consider in evaluating responses.

Carin, Arthur A., and Sund, Robert B., *Developing Questioning Techniques: A Self-Concept Approach.* New York: Charles E. Merrill, 1971. The entire book contains helpful, practical suggestions for making discussion sessions popular and meaningful.

Sebesta, Sam Leaton, and Iverson, William J., *Literature for Thursday's Child.* Chicago: Science Research Associates, 1975. Part III contains a plan for integrating questions and activities of different types and levels.

Ruddell, Robert B., *Reading-Language Instruction: Innovative Practices.* Englewood Cliffs, N.J.: Prentice Hall, 1974. Chapter 11 includes transcripts and a guide to developing questioning strategies and promoting verbal interaction.

Oral and Written Composition

FROM RESPONSE TO COMPOSITION

Children and young people have much to say. They enjoy talking about what they have read. Their enthusiasm goes beyond the act of reading and answering a few questions about a literary selection.

Young readers may enjoy *retelling* a story, thus transforming the written form into oral language. They are likely to add a phrase here, change a word there, or *infer* a scrap of conversation or a detail of setting. Such alterations may not indicate a faulty memory at all, but rather show the teller's ability to reconstruct literature in imagination. Young readers may *extrapolate* from, or extend, a story. They may tell what might have happened after the story ended, or how it might have been different in another setting or situation. They may also relate the selection to their own experience, and thus *interpret* its meaning in terms of their own lives.

All of these types of responses have appeared in the oral and written responses of children and young people as they reacted to literature.[3,4] When such responses comprise a group of sentences with a central topic or purpose, they become a *composition*. A composition may be oral or written. It may be the product of an entire class, as when students dictate a paragraph to the teacher. It may be the product of a pair of students working together to stimulate each other's ideas and to share the speaking or writing task. A composition may also be done by an individual who either writes it down or dictates it into a tape recorder or to another person.

Preparing for Composition. The preparation process for composition should begin orally, even if the result is to be a written product. An oral warm-up stimulates ideas through interaction. It permits immediate feedback and the chance to try out an idea before taking the effort and time to shape it completely.

At first, during the oral warm-up, students may use brainstorming techniques. Working in pairs or small groups, they are encouraged to say anything that comes to mind relevant to the assignment. Later in the warm-up, they review and evaluate what has been said.

It is good to remember, however, that some students work better alone during the warm-up time. These students need a period of quiet time to work uninterrupted on their ideas.

Where and When to Write. The time and place for composition may vary according to your needs and those of your students. A writing corner, partially separated from the rest of the classroom, helps give some children inspiration and privacy for their task. Others are quite happy to remain with the group, perhaps gaining confidence through numbers. Some sit "properly" at their desks while others may capture the flow of ideas in a more informal, relaxed posture.

Some teachers like to assign a composition project, encourage warm-up for fluency, and then set the entire class to the oral or written composition task. While stu-

---

3. Alan C. Purves with Victoria Rippere, *Elements of Writing About a Literary Work: A Study of Response to Literature* (Urbana, Illinois: National Council of Teachers of English, 1968).

4. James R. Squire, *The Responses of Adolescents While Reading Four Short Stories* (Urbana, Illinois: National Council of Teachers of English, 1964).

dents work, the teacher circulates about the room offering individual help.

Other teachers make composition an ongoing process. Students may work on the assigned task at almost any time in the day. This plan has the advantage of permitting children to seize the moment of inspiration and work on an independent schedule. Its results are excitingly described in a classic book about creative composition, *They All Want To Write*, by Alvina Treut Burrows and three other teachers who experimented with the plan over a period of four years.[5]

THE ORAL COMPOSITION PROCESS

In the primary grades, oral composition is often spontaneous. For example, suppose a second-grade class had just read James Marshall's humorous story "Split Pea Soup," in which George is faced with eating his least favorite food every time he visits his friend Martha. The teacher may prepare the class for a composition assignment with a question such as, "What do you think Martha did the next time George came to visit her?" After inviting a number of answers, the teacher may suggest that the group compose a story about George's next visit. The group decides on one of the answers gathered from the discussion as story material.

Now the oral story process begins. If oral composition is a new experience, you and the group may be satisfied with a few sentences describing the chosen incident. There is no "editing" and no rejection of ideas. It is more important to get each group member to contribute something to the story. As a follow-up, some children

may perform the story as a puppet show (see page T43) while others illustrate the story.

Refining the Story.   Gradually these spontaneous story-making sessions can be modified and enriched. After the warm-up, two or three children can choose one of the story ideas and prepare to tell it before the group. Alternatively, the entire class can continue to work on a story, but this time you might add some oral editing skillfully and unobtrusively.

Suppose, for example, that the group has just read "The Garden," one of Arnold Lobel's Frog and Toad stories (Level Two). Now the group is composing a story about what happens after Toad's seeds begin to grow in his garden. A main happening has been agreed upon: the seeds will grow into such large flowers that Toad's house will be covered. One child suggests as a first sentence for the story, "The flowers got so big that Toad couldn't find his house when he came home from the store."

Now the teacher can help extend and refine the story, "Why had Toad gone to the store in the first place?"

Student 1: He went to buy a watering can.
Student 2: He bought some fast-grow pills he saw on television.
Student 3: A dog on TV said, "Give your flowers a treat with Quick Grow!"
Teacher: Now let's go back and start the story.
Student 1: Next day, Toad went to the store. He bought some pills to make his flowers grow. Then he bought a watering can.
Student 4: When he came back, he said, "Where's my house? All I can see is flowers!"
Student 3: A flower said, "Get out of here! I need that place where you are so I can grow."

5. Alvina Treut Burrows, et al. *They All Want to Write: Written English in the Elementary Schools,* 3d ed. (New York: Holt, Rinehart & Winston, 1964).

Teacher: What did the flower look like—the one that said that?

Student 3: It was pink and it had a big tongue hanging out. . . .

As the story continues, the teacher can ask questions to help students organize and amplify it. There must be a give-and-take: encouragement to take risks, to try out ideas, and to alter the story when a "better" way is discovered.

THE WRITTEN COMPOSITION

If the story is deemed a success by its makers, the oral composition may merge into writing. In the primary grades, the teacher may write the story on the chalkboard or on a large note pad or a sheet of newsprint as the students watch. Later the story can be copied onto a ditto master and duplicated. Each student can receive a copy to illustrate or to practice reading aloud.

Writing a First Draft. The oral composition may also be transcribed by the students themselves. Many children move early toward independence in writing skills so that, after the initial warm-up, they can proceed on their own. Here, as in earlier stages, encourage risk taking and trial and error.

It is best *not* to ask that the first draft of a story, a poem, or a nonfiction composition be a finished product. Instead suggest that students begin writing by simply "filling a page" with attempts to start the composition in an interesting manner, with thoughts that need to be jotted down lest they be forgotten in the final writing, or with scraps of conversation or detail. Then, instruct students to prepare the first draft by writing on every other line, so that revisions can be made using the empty in-between lines.

Students should be free to scratch out and scribble in; they should be encouraged to attempt spelling words that they want to use, whether they can spell them correctly or not. Such use of "invented spellings" helps students achieve fluency and leaves them free to concentrate on expressing their ideas. Neatness and correctness are reserved for the final draft.

EDITING THE COMPOSITION

The trial and error of the composition process is a form of editing. When a first draft of a composition, oral or written, is planned and then reviewed for practice and improvement, editing is taking place.

Editing needs to be taught—and taught gradually. It is self-criticism, but criticism with a constructive purpose: to go over one's original creation with a listener's ear or a reader's eye to figure out how the creation can be improved. Editing is not correcting. It is reshaping, deciding whether a scene in a story ought to be changed in some way or whether a paragraph in a report belongs somewhere else. It is revising sentences and words that lack force or fail to say what is intended. For example, the teacher who asked the student to describe the flower in the discussion about Toad's garden was helping the child expand, and hence edit, his or her first oral draft. The child's original version, "A flower said, 'Get out of here!'" might therefore become "A big pink flower stuck its tongue out and said, 'Get out of here!'"

Developing Editing Skills at Intermediate and Upper Grades. At the intermediate grade levels and above, the skills of editing may be more directly taught. A series of questions like the following, organized by category, can be used according to what is to be stressed in a lesson.

Editing Story Structure.
- Does your story start at an exciting place?
- Would a certain scene be more interesting if you expanded it?
- Is there a scene that is too long?
- Would some of the story be lost if the scene were shortened?

Editing Conversation.
- Does the dialogue "sound" like spoken language?
- Is there conversation in your story that is just "filler" and could be left out?
- Is there a place where conversation needs to be added to increase suspense or to move the story along?

Editing Sentences.
- Is there a place in your story where you can help your composition flow by using one of these connector words or phrases: *so, therefore, if–then, because, since*?
- Can one sentence be combined with another to make the meaning clearer? (Note: Language arts textbooks provide sequences and practice in sentence *combining* and *expanding*. The emphasis in editing may be placed on the specific skills concurrently taught in the language arts text used in the class.)

Editing Words.
- Can you make your writing style more direct by striking out empty words such as *very* and *a lot*?
- Can you use a more specific descriptive term by finding a synonym in a thesaurus?

At upper grade levels, students may be introduced to proofreaders' marks such as those used for deletion, insertion, and new paragraph, along with the term *stet*, which means "do not make the change indicated." These aids to editing are in most dictionaries.

Correcting for a Final Draft. To insist that everything spoken or written be perfect in mechanics can be stultifying, yet correct spelling, punctuation, capitalization, paragraphing, and all the other rudiments of acceptable form must be taught.

The best way to teach mechanics without hampering fluency is to distinguish between *process* and *product*. During the composition process, emphasis should be placed upon creating—originating, exploring, and elaborating upon ideas. When the process yields a product that the student wants others to hear or read in finished form, the rules of correctness need to be followed.

Here are some helpful ways to teach mechanics:

1. *Have the students tape-record their speeches or hand in written first drafts of compositions.* You can listen to the recordings or correct the drafts, offering suggestions for improvement before the students present their work in final form.

2. *Encourage self-criticism.* Each student may be given an alphabetized list of words frequently used but sometimes misspelled. A recent source for such a list is Robert L. Hillerich's *A Writing Vocabulary of Elementary Children*.[6] A class dictionary is also a useful tool.

3. *Emphasize punctuation and handwriting when students prepare final copies of written compositions.*

Polishing the Oral Composition.
Oral compositions can be practiced with the aid of a partner who acts as director. The partner may suggest changes in delivery, identifying places where pace and force may be varied, correcting pronunciation, and offering an opinion about the

---

6. Robert L. Hillerich, *A Writing Vocabulary of Elementary Children* (Springfield, Illinois: Charles C. Thomas, 1978).

general effect of the speech upon the audience. Directors should be cautioned, however, to make their criticisms helpful not only by pointing out what could be improved, but also by commenting on what is good about their partners' composition and the interpretation of it.

Whether students create oral or written compositions, the values of the composition process are many. Among these should be an increased appreciation both for good literature and for the skillful authors who have created it.

Additional Readings

Lewis, Claudia. *A Big Bite of the World: Children's Creative Writing*. Englewood Cliffs, N.J.: Prentice-Hall, 1979. Examples and theory of a composition program used in Bank Street College of Education and Portland State University, involving children from the ages of three through twelve.

Tiedt, Sidney W., and Tiedt, Iris M. *Language Arts Activities for the Classroom*. Boston: Allyn & Bacon, 1978. Separate chapters give numerous examples and teaching ideas for writing, spelling, and listening, as well as ideas for using poetry and fiction in the language arts program.

Stewig, John Warren. *Read to Write: Using Children's Literature as a Springboard for Teaching Writing*. 2d ed. New York: Holt, Rinehart & Winston, 1980.

Smith, James A., and Park, Dorothy M. *Word Music and Word Magic: Children's Literature Methods*. Boston: Allyn & Bacon, 1977. A wealth of examples and techniques show integration of the best in modern and classical children's literature with the entire school curriculum, including composition.

Interpretive Reading and Dramatization

INTERPRETIVE ORAL READING

Sharing Interpretations. To interpret a story or poem well requires practice and concentration. The interpretive activity should follow careful silent reading of the selection and incorporate insights gained through discussion. Interpretive oral reading usually implies an audience—one or more listeners to whom the reader presents his or her interpretation.

The key to interpretive reading is *concentration*. Readers must learn to concentrate on finding the image and the feeling they want to impart and to work steadfastly toward that goal in their oral reading. Here, then, are seven suggestions you can make to help the students in your class read aloud interpretively:

1. *Find a selection, a stanza from a poem, or a scene from a story that you really want to read aloud to others.*

2. *Figure out why you have selected it.* If it is funny, what makes it funny? The language? The action? The surprise? If it is scary, what makes it so? Frightening words? A gradual build-up to a big scare?

3. *Now visualize the images or the pictures behind the words.* If you "see" the pictures in your mind as you read the selection aloud, your listeners will see them too. Sometimes it helps to tell yourself all about the pictures you imagine. Add ideas that the author did not tell you, using your imagination as you read.

4. *If the story or poem has action, try imitating the action as you practice reading.* Then leave out the movement and try to show the action with just your voice.

5. *Practice reading until you do not have to look at the words all the time.* Then read the selection to an empty chair three meters (approximately ten feet) or more away from you. Look often at the chair as you read. If the chair were alive, could it hear you? Would it like hearing the selection the way you are reading it?

6. For intermediate and upper grades: *Identify the purpose of each scene in a story or stanza in a poem.* Write one phrase that tells that purpose, for example, *to scare*, *to surprise*, or *to win sympathy*. Then, keep that purpose in mind as you read. Write the purpose on a sign and put the sign on your practice chair. Stop in the middle of your practice reading and ask yourself, ''Am I reading to show that purpose?''

7. *After you have the pictures and the purpose in mind, try experimenting with the volume and pace of your voice.* Vary your voice from almost a whisper to almost a shout, from very fast to very slow. Then use some of this variety to help your listeners get the purpose in your reading.

Improving Oral Reading. Interpretive oral reading improves with praise if the praise is specific. ''You read that with a great deal of expression'' is not specific enough, it does not tell the reader what he or she did effectively. A more useful comment might be ''I could hear the ghost rattling the dishes when you read that scene'' or ''I felt the sorrow of the man and woman when the girl told them she had to leave.''

Interpretive oral reading also improves with good models. Most communities contain good models, so you may want to arrange readings by amateur or professional actors, senior citizens or parents with time and talent for reading aloud. The request to ''come and read to us'' may bring surprising, pleasing results.

CHORAL SPEAKING

Drawing Upon the Flow and Feel of Words.
''Star light, star bright, first star I've seen tonight. . . .'' These simple, clear words, memory-cued by rhythm and rhyme, invite instant playback. The invitation ''Now say it with me!'' puts the choral-speaking mechanism in motion.

Almost every rhymed and metered poem in the primary grades can be enhanced through choral speaking. In addition, shared speaking encourages participation without risk. Shyness, fear of making mistakes, and the embarrassment of forgetting lines are all overcome as one speaks with the group.

This technique is also an aid to reading, particularly when used in the early years. As students recite together, they may rely partly on memory and partly on print to guide them. In this way, the ''difficult'' words become familiar in print.

Avoiding the Sing-Song Pitfall.
In choral reading, metered poetry may begin to sound ''sing-song,'' a mere exercise in reciting rhythm without the intended interpretation of meaning. One way to avoid this pitfall is *not* to confine intermediate- and upper-grade choral reading to rhymed and metered poetry. An alternative is to let the sing-song pleasure of a metered poem run half its course, and then begin to introduce variety into the reading. Another is to concentrate on the poem's meaning. You might begin by reading a few lines of a poem and asking questions like these: ''Who is saying these lines? How should the lines be said? In a puzzled voice? In a sad voice? With a laughing tone? What is happening in the poem? How can we show this feeling with our voices?'' Such attention to meaning, even with nonsense poetry, will help direct the rhythm and sound away from a sing-song pattern and toward vocal variety in pace and volume.

Another way to avoid sing-song interpretations is to divide the choral reading so that *all* speakers do not read *all* of the lines. Some lines can be read in unison by all speakers, but some will be read by a subgroup or by one speaker.

PUPPETRY

Puppet shows hold fascination for children and adults. Students who a moment ago complained "I can't think of what to say" are suddenly released when "it is the puppets who do the talking."

Construction of Puppets. In order to leave time for the production, select one of the following easy-to-make puppets.

1. *Hand puppets*. A simple hand puppet may be no more than an old sock stretched over the hand and adjusted so that the curved palm of the hand opens and closes like a mouth. The face of the hand puppet can be dabbed on with tempera paint or constructed from yarn, buttons, and sewn-on shapes of cloth.

2. *Stick puppets*. A stick puppet may consist of a painted or cut-paper face on a flat surface such as a paper plate stapled or pasted on the end of a tongue depressor.

3. *Fist puppets*. A fist puppet is more elaborate than those mentioned above. The fist puppet's head is modeled out of papier-maché or other lightweight material, such as cotton or crushed paper with heavy paper covering. Features are applied with poster paint. The puppet's eyes should be larger than life to provide emphasis. A cardboard cylinder big enough to fit over the index finger is embedded at the neck of the puppet. The puppet's costume can be cloth that is cut and sewn to be gathered at the puppet's neck, with sleeves that fit over the puppeteer's thumb and fifth finger.

Practice and Performance. Give students time to experiment with their newly constructed puppets—to play with voice and movement. When they are ready to perform, they may present the puppet show as Story Theater, where one or more readers read the story while puppeteers manipulate the puppets to show the action. The puppeteers may also perform the story on their own, using creative dramatics techniques to improvise dialogue and gesture. Finally, scripts may be selected or prepared: some students may read the speeches while other students manipulate the puppets; or the puppeteers may speak the puppets' dialogue as they manipulate them.

READERS THEATRE

In Readers Theatre—the term is usually spelled that way, without an apostrophe—students read orally from scripts that are often based on selections from literature. Play scripts, then, are especially suitable for reading with this technique, since characters' speeches are already indicated. The technique is also adaptable for use with stories and poems that contain considerable direct conversation.

Specialists in the Readers Theatre technique indicate that selections may be abridged or occasionally paraphrased for script purposes. They warn, however, that scripts are to be used only for specific performance; to circulate scripts extensively or to use them for wide public performance is against copyright law.

How It Works. Similar to actors in a play, the performers in Readers Theatre "take roles"; they speak lines assigned to characters or to one or more narrators. But unlike actors, Readers Theatre performers do not move about a stage; they hold scripts in hand or place them on music stands or desks. A few gestures and changes in position are permitted if these help the interpretation, but the real effect of the literary selection must come from the readers' oral interpretation of characters and narration. Hence the suggestions for interpretive oral reading (page T41) are appropriate for Readers Theatre practice as well.

The prospect of a Readers Theatre performance is highly motivating to students. Once roles are assigned, they do not need to be told to practice their oral reading. They will do so on their own, especially when they can practice with a partner or a "dialogue director" who can give instant feedback on whether or not the character is "coming through" in the reading.

The Importance of the Director. The presentation can be improved by a good director who tells the readers how an audience might receive their efforts. Who should be the director? A student? The teacher? A parent volunteer? Any one of these will do if he or she can bravely but not threateningly stop the rehearsal at almost any point to offer advice: "I didn't *hear* how angry the two trolls were when Prince Lini refused them. Try that again" (*Half a Kingdom*, Level 4). Of course, the director must find a balance between expecting too much in a performance and permitting flaccid, unthinking reading. Students respond to direction that asks for, but does not demand, a lively, varied interpretation.

Finally, the finished production may be performed for an audience. Performers may sit or stand side by side, facing the audience, or they may position themselves so that two opposing characters face each other, the narrators off to one side and slightly closer to the audience. The audience, the performance area, and the likely arrangement of readers should be decided upon before final rehearsals begin, so that the readers feel they are working toward a well-planned, polished performance.

STORY THEATER

Interpretive oral reading is combined with "acting out" in Story Theater. One or more students read aloud the selection, which should be a story or a poem with plenty of action. Simultaneously, a group of "players" performs the actions described in the reading. In addition, players may sometimes act as scenery. For example, several may portray a wall, a tree, or the window of a house.

How It Works. Story Theater begins with attentive reading and discussion of the story to be presented. Movement, or mime, can be encouraged as a natural extension of inference questions: "Show us how the lizard moves his head from side to side. Show how the hawk soars over the land, looking for the ring" ("The Wedding of the Hawk," Level 6). Roles are assigned or chosen by volunteers. Players develop their parts as they listen to the oral readers' rendition of the story; oral readers practice their skill until they can vary their pace to accommodate the pace of the players. The final performance, then, is a combination of oral reading and mimed action.

After its completion, the performance should be evaluated by the participants, using questions such as the following: *Which segments in the reading gave life to the story? What did the players do to make certain actions vivid? When a player was present but not specifically mentioned in a moment of action, what did he or she do? Did the player* freeze, *standing still so that attention was directed to the action, or did the player* react *to what was happening?*

Would a different response have been more effective?

The critique, or evaluation, may be followed by a second performance, and students may then note improvements.

Choosing Appropriate Selections.

For primary-grade children, Story Theater works well with nursery rhymes and other simple action poems. It seems especially suited to folk tales that highlight action and do not contain a great deal of dialogue. Intermediate- and upper-level students, however, may wish to experiment with Story Theater productions in which players speak lines of dialogue.

CREATIVE DRAMATICS/ IMPROVISATION

A story or a poem is read. During the discussion that follows, the teacher says, "*Show* us what you mean." A student gestures, mimes a series of actions, or speaks a line in a certain way to demonstrate a character or a description. From such a simple, brief beginning can come the activity often called *creative dramatics*. Creative dramatics is especially valuable for developing skills of inference, as students must infer the actions and motives that characters would be likely to display within the framework of the story. The inferring activity shapes and implements both action and motive. It thus goes a step beyond the more passive inference brought forward through discussion.

First Steps.   Creative dramatics develops gradually. Begin by having students identify *one* crucial scene they would like to play. Then have them "try on" characters and develop gestures, facial expressions, and a manner of speech for each. Lines of dialogue may be quoted directly from the story, but memorizing should not get in the way of the playing. Instead, encourage players to *improvise* dialogue in the spirit of the story and scene.

Once the improvisation is under way, there may be a tendency for the scene to go on and on. If this happens, stop the action. (A signal from you, such as the single word "Curtain," can be used to stop the action without embarrassing anyone.) Immediately ask students to evaluate the playing: "What was strong in the playing? What seemed to be going wrong?" At this point, ask the group, players and observers alike, to reread the scene.

Insight into Character.   Geraldine Siks, an expert on creative dramatics procedure, offers a further suggestion: Have each player identify first the *big purpose* of his or her character in terms of the entire story, and then the character's *little purpose* in the scene that is being played. In addition, character traits and emotions should be discussed.[7] During this discussion, the focus should be on the characters, not the players. Say, for example: "The old man must show that he is terrified of the sea monster," not "You should act more terrified when you look at the sea monster."

Following evaluation, the scene should be replayed. Further evaluation should note any improvements in the playing.

The Need for Brief but Frequent Sessions.   The single-scene sessions should be brief, perhaps no longer than ten minutes in primary grades and fifteen minutes in intermediate and upper grades. Frequent sessions, perhaps two per week, are recommended by most experts as the best way to move from creative dramatics to meaningful dramatic interpretation.

---

7. Geraldine Brain Siks, *Drama with Children* (New York: Harper & Row, 1977), p. 119.

From Scene to Story. At all levels, dramatizing a single scene can lead to playing an entire story once the improvisation process runs smoothly. When an entire story is dramatized, pace and structure become more important than ever. The story must progress without having dialogue or action distract from its central focus. Winifred Ward, perhaps the best-known expert in the field of creative dramatics in schools, advises that planners and players must "concentrate on essentials," shortening or omitting scenes that contribute to the written story but do not move the drama forward. Scenes themselves often require "tightening," which involves highlighting the essential movement and dialogue while omitting the nonessential. Ward's basic evaluation question at this point is "Did the scene *move*?"[8] Attention must also be directed to the clear presentation of the story's problems in an early scene and to the build-up through successive scenes to a climax and solution.

Role Playing. An extension of creative dramatics is *role playing*, a technique that requires extrapolation. In role playing, a story is read up to the point at which a problem is encountered but not solved. Students discuss what the main characters will do about the situation. Roles are assigned, possible solutions are enacted, and the results are evaluated by asking, "Is this what the main characters *would* do? Is this what they *should* do?"

One of the values of role playing is evident when students return to the story to read the author's solution to the problem they have resolved. They do so with heightened interest, for they have taken an active role in predicting the story's outcome.

PLAY PRODUCTION

Informal Presentations. In the classroom, a play script may be presented informally without scenery, costumes, or memorization, and with minimal movement. An informal presentation provides practice in characterization and timing. It also improves speaking skills, especially if readers must project their voices to an audience. The informal presentation can be enhanced if it is recorded on tape as a "radio play" with background music and sound effects. The tape may then be played for the readers' enjoyment and evaluation.

Formal Productions. Formal production based on a play script requires much more time and planning, and it deserves an audience. It may also require a budget. Still, the excitement of a formal production of a play often makes the effort worthwhile. So, too, do the other rewards: the literary learning that results from extended close work with the play script, the confidence that arises from successfully portraying characters and incidents, and the poise that comes with performing in a company before an audience.

Preparing Young Students for Play Productions. Students at the primary level need informal experience in drama before attempting a formal play production. Both Story Theater and creative dramatics should come first. Then, when a play script is before the students and the decision is made to present it as a play, they need to become aware of its requirements. Maxine McSweeny[9] reported one group's suggestions for play performance, which were written on the chalkboard by their teacher:

---

8. Winifred Ward, *Playmaking with Children from Kindergarten Through Junior High School*, 2d ed. (New York: Appleton-Century-Crofts, 1957), p. 138.

9. Maxine McSweeny, *Creative Children's Theatre for Home, School, Church, and Playground* (Cranbury, N.J.: A. S. Barnes, 1974), p. 131.

- Know exactly what to say and do. [They can't make it up in front of an audience.]
- Act so the audience can see what they do.
- Speak so the audience can understand what they say.
- Make the play's story live for the audience.

Suggestions for a Successful Production. Once a class has had some experience with formal play production on a small scale, the following suggestions may help to guide more extensive productions.

1. *Make sure the class has had sufficient experience in oral interpretation and movement before they try to perform a play that requires extensive dialogue and a succession of scenes.*

2. *Make sure the class* likes *the play script.* Talk it over. Ask them to explain the dramatic appeal: "What might an audience like about this play?"

3. *Hold try-outs for all facets of the production, not just for acting roles.* Ask for volunteers to make scenery (drawn, painted, constructed, or hung as a backdrop), to be in charge of props, or to act as dialogue coaches. The actors themselves must be selected carefully, of course. Have them try out by improvisation rather than by reading lines. Ask pairs of students to assume the characters from the play and then to compose speeches and movements to fit a particular scene.

4. *With class participation, make a schedule for rehearsals.* The first session should consist of reading lines, with attention to oral interpretation of character. The second session should begin the *blocking* of action, determining characters' movements about the stage in each scene. In general, movement must be motivated, and a character should not move while another is speaking.

"Stage business"—the use of props and gestures—is included in the blocking of action. At this point actors may carry scripts but they should also devote attention to memorizing lines. Subsequent sessions give practice, scene by scene, in dialogue and action.

5. *When planning scenery, costumes, and lighting, suggest rather than strive for actuality.* Setting may be suggested by scenery sketched on wrapping paper or merely by a backdrop consisting of a curtain or drape. An item of costume, such as a hat or an appropriate jacket, can suffice to designate a character. Lighting need not require footlights or spotlights, but the playing area should be clearly visible to an audience. The playing area itself can be a cleared area in the classroom if a raised stage is not available.

6. *Set aside time for a* dress rehearsal— *a session in which the entire production receives a run-through without interruption.* During this final rehearsal, the director may keep notes so that he or she can comment on the production afterward. The comments should be mainly positive, to encourage the players and crew to do their best. If the performance is to run smoothly, few changes should be made in the production at this point.

7. *Plan to present a formal production before an audience.* Besides offering a means for appreciating the considerable efforts of the cast, crew, and director, the production of a play is intended to provide entertainment for others. Some groups plan more than one performance, for increased experience before an audience.

A Word About Royalties. Some plays, if presented formally, require payment of royalties. Be sure to check the title and copyright pages of a play script for a royalty statement before deciding to put the script into production.

A Sense of Accomplishment. Allot time when the production is over for evaluating what was learned, what was especially satisfying, and what might be done "next time" to make the production process flow more smoothly. Teachers and other adults involved need to remember that play production in schools is for education, appreciation, and pleasure. A good question to consider is this: "Ten years from now will this play be recalled by my students with pleasure and a sense of real accomplishment?"

Let it also be remembered that theater experience with literature is *direct* experience with literature. As author Tove Jansson has a wise character say in *Moomin's Summer Madness*, "A theatre is the most important sort of house in the world, because that's where people are shown what they could be if they wanted, and what they'd like to be if they dared to, and what they really are."[10]

Additional Readings

Provenmire, E. Kingsley. *Choral Speaking and the Verse Choir*. Cranbury, N.J.: A. S. Barnes, 1975. Definitions, procedures, and materials for voice choir are presented, with discussion focused on each age level.

Coger, Lesley Irene, and White, Melvin R. *Readers Theatre Handbook: A Dramatic Approach to Literature*. Rev. ed. Glenview, Ill.: Scott, Foresman, 1973. Definitions, procedures, and "rules" for successful Readers Theatre productions, with helpful case studies of how the procedures have succeeded in schools.

---

10. Tove Jansson, *Moomin's Summer Madness* trans. Ernest Benn, Ltd. (New York: Avon Books, 1955), pp. 105–106.

McCaslin, Nellie. *Creative Drama in the Classroom*, 3d ed. New York: Longman, 1980. This up-to-date edition gives reasons for using pantomime, improvisation, and creative dramatics. It is rich in examples of how to use drama in the classroom, especially for interpretations of poetry and other literary forms.

Visual Arts, Music, and Literature

ART ACTIVITIES

The visual arts offer teachers and students a great variety of activities: drawing and painting, paper cutting, sculpting and modeling, constructing and printmaking. Any one of these can stir the students' imaginations and provide them with a visual means of responding to literature.

The teacher's choice of which art activity will enhance a literary experience can be guided by class discussions of a particular selection. For example, if the discussion focuses on the *setting*, then students might sketch the setting or visualize it through collage. As they reread a description of a setting in a story or a poem, urge the students to develop a mental image. Then using pencil, crayon, pastel, charcoal, or another sketching instrument, they can sketch quickly on paper the scene in their imaginations. Later, details may be added and the scene may be finished with tempera paint, water color, chalk, or another medium.

Characters in literature also may fire the imagination. Following a discussion of a main character's traits, invite students to model that character from clay. Encourage them *not* to try to represent how the character looked, but rather what the character was like and the impression that character made upon the readers. Finished clay figures, dried or baked in a kiln, can be displayed against a painted or constructed background of the story's setting. Students in the upper grades might sculpt figures from plaster of paris blocks.

In addition to individual art projects, you may sometimes wish to encourage group projects in response to literature. For example, students could create a mural or a large map of a "journey" story, labeling each place and major event in the story. Students also could make an *accordion book* by the following method: the class identifies the main events in the story; each student sketches one of the events; the sketches are arranged in order and then connected by loose stitching or metal rings. The result is a visual display of the story sequence.

MUSIC ACTIVITIES

The rhythms and sounds of words have their counterparts in the rhythms and sounds of music. Poems with strong rhythms or pleasant-sounding lines can inspire song making. To create songs from poems, have students read a poem several times to bring out the rhythm, phrasing, and mood. Use choral speaking techniques to do this. Then have students experiment with beat and sample melodies, progressing line-by-line through the poem. When the final song version is put together, tape the melody or quickly notate it above a written version of the poem.

Musical instruments can be used to create sounds that will heighten the mood for oral reading or any performance of literature. A "signature tune," for instance, may announce the entrance of each character in the telling of a folk tale. Such tunes can be composed on a homemade xylophone, recorder, or kalimba. To stress the rhythm in a poem, use rhythm sticks, various types of drums, sand blocks, and maracas. Musical instruments may also be used to help establish the setting of a story or a play.

Listening to music may also enhance literary appreciation. To seek a literal tie between a literary selection and a musical selection is unnecessary. For example, no composer has written a symphony, ballet, or specific program music to accompany the Norwegian folk tale "The Three Billy Goats Gruff" (Level 1, Reader), yet children can find the troll and the setting of the drama in numerous works of the Norwegian composer Edvard Greig. Played before, during, and after the reading of a selection, such music adds impact while developing the students' listening abilities.

These are only a few of the boundless opportunities to promote literary appreciation and response through the visual arts and music. Boundless, too, is the pleasure to be gained.

Additional Readings

Gaitskell, Charles D., and Hurwitz, Al. *Children and Their Art*. 3d ed. New York: Harcourt Brace Jovanovich, 1975. This book presents a synthesis of child development and art development. It includes many examples that help explain how to encourage child development with art education.

Taylor, Gail Cohen. "Music in Language Arts Instruction." *Language Arts* 58, no. 3 (March 1981): 363–367. This review of recent writing on the topic includes a section on music as an aid to story enjoyment and comprehension as well as a list of resources for teachers.

Poetry and the Teacher
Myra Cohn Livingston

I am myself,
of all my atom parts I am the sum.
And out of my blood and my brain
I make my own interior weather,
my own sun and rain.
Imprint my mark upon the world,
whatever I shall become.

Eve Merriam, "Thumbprint"

ROBERT FROST has written that a poem "begins in delight and ends in wisdom." The Irish poet James Stephens tells us that "What the heart knows today the head will understand tomorrow." In these words both poets suggest one of the most meaningful ways of introducing children to poetry: to infect with *delight,* stress the *joy,* approach through the *heart,* and know that wisdom and understanding will follow. It makes all the difference.

Children grow into poetry, beginning with Mother Goose. From the first time they hear rhyming verses that tell a small story, that play with words, that move along with bouncing rhythms, that stress rhyme, they are affirming a basic need to listen with both heart and movement—to respond with pleasure.

Jack be nimble,
Jack be quick,
Jack jump over
The candlestick.

Even nonsense poems allow them to test their own knowledge of what is true and what is not, to improve their self-images, and to be able to laugh both at others and at themselves:

Far and few, far and few,
 Are the lands where the Jumblies live:
Their heads are green, and their hands
 are blue;
And they went to sea in a sieve.

Edward Lear, "The Jumblies"

New discoveries, thoughts, dreams, widely ranging emotions surround children as they grow up. Poetry mirrors their experiences through a more sophisticated handling of imagery, rhythm, and sound. What distinguishes poetry from other forms of literature is a rhythm that almost invites our bodies to move, our fingers to tap, our feet to dance; combinations of words that make us wish to repeat them aloud; rhymes, oftentimes, that encourage us to make up our own series of sounds; and a sort of irresistible music that engages heart, mind, and body. From the simplest folk rhyme to the ballad, from the traditional to the most experimental contemporary poem, poetry gives children room where their emotions and imaginations may run free.

DISCOVERING POETRY

The delight of poetry is in discovery: a new image, a different way of looking, the pleasure of words and rhythms used well, a humorous idea, an eccentric person, a striking metaphor. The delight is in the freedom to choose from among so many kinds of poems the ones that speak to us. The delight is in becoming familiar with riddles and limericks, haiku and counting rhymes, ballads and shape poems. The delight remains so long as children are able to come to a poem and find something of themselves and their world mirrored, extended, or even stretched. The delight allows them to act out the stories in pantomime or dance, to sculpt, to illustrate, to chant the words aloud, alone or with others, to try writing poems of their own, to respond in individual ways to the poetry they hear and read.

In the ten books of the ODYSSEY series, teachers will find verse and poetry to bring delight and pleasure. Here are traditional verses that have long been favorites of young readers, juxtaposed with verse by contemporary poets who write for today's young people. A mixture of light and serious verse spanning centuries and cultures has been selected within the thematic strands to afford a wide choice for both teacher and student. It may certainly happen that some of the selections will not appeal to every child or teacher. All of us hear a different tune. Some enjoy rhyming verse and ordered meter, while others prefer a freer, more open approach to poetry. Humorous verse, limericks, and riddles appeal to some; poetry with a more serious tone, a different mood, to others. Fortunately there are enough poems for all. Both teachers and students should always feel free to pick and choose what is meaningful to them as individuals.

It is here, I believe, that the wisdom and understanding of which Robert Frost and James Stephens spoke become important. Wisdom is *not* the message given by a poem to a reader; wisdom is *not* didacticism cajoling, exhorting, or instructing the reader of a poem to behave in a certain fashion; wisdom is *not* high-flown sentiments in lofty diction. Nor is wisdom

achieved by tearing apart a poem to find what figures of speech, what symbolism it may contain. Rather, wisdom is acquired by knowing that as we read poetry we grow in understanding. Wisdom is found by relating our thoughts and emotions as individuals to ourselves and to others about us, to other cultures, other centuries, other places. Wisdom comes in knowing that the best poetry has something to say for each of us if we first make the commitment to find the delight. Wisdom also implies that *comprehending* is not nearly so important as *apprehending*. As John Ciardi has pointed out, it is important that we never ask ''*What* does a poem mean?'' but rather ''*How* does a poem mean?'' For Ciardi, the skillful combination of idea, form, words, and rhythm separates real poetry from mere pleasantries put into verse form.

Most likely we will not want to speak to children about methods of delighting or wisdom and understanding. What we can do is try to show them that poetry is part of life. Poetry has something to say about the way we view ourselves, our world, and everything in that world from a drop of rain to mirrors in the Fun House to our feelings about ourselves. Poetry can be funny, it can be sad. It is not, as many believe, a unit of study we get once a year filled with iambic pentameter and some poems to memorize.

Because of the increasing number of fine poetry anthologies available, it is possible for teachers in all grades to relate poetry to almost any subject. History might be studied using some of the folk poetry of America. Numerous poems deal with science and math. The ODYSSEY Teacher's Editions offer a wide variety of suggestions for integrating poetry with other arts—painting, dancing, creative writing, and dramatics, to name just a few.

Our most difficult job as teachers today may well lie in the need to elicit imaginative responses. In a world that promotes an unusual amount of passivity, reliance on mass media, and a great deal of programmed response, teachers need to touch the imagination of each child, to encourage this individual reaction to what is heard or read. In a single classroom there may be but a handful of children who respond to a given poem, but this reaction should be praised and nurtured. What happens when a poem and the right listener, the right reader, come together can be magic.

SHARING POETRY IN THE CLASSROOM

It will come as no surprise to teachers that few children today hear nursery rhymes at home. The classroom may well be the first place children hear poetry, and the teacher may well be the first person who reads poetry to them aloud. No matter what age or level of the students, poetry should be read aloud as often as possible.

Many of the poems in the ten ODYSSEY readers are suitable for individual and choral reading. Students can organize group readings of poems or memorize them for the joy of it. Many balk at the idea of memorization, but if a student especially likes a poem, the results can be wonderful! Whole classes have put on poetry programs to entertain other classes until the entire school becomes infected with the joy of performing. Again, if imagination is encouraged by the teacher, the students benefit not only from their personal response to poetry but grow with their hearts and minds to bring its enjoyment to others. Here are a few suggestions to help you get started.

1. *Choose poems you like and those you think your class will like.* Teachers cannot elicit enthusiasm for work they themselves do not enjoy. Be aware that riddles, limericks, and light verse will always be received well, but that other kinds of poetry will help young people grow in their perceptions and relationships with others.

2. *Encourage students to find verses and poems and share them with the class.*

3. *Experiment with different ways of reading the sounds and rhythms of poems.* One way to read a poem is to read each line as a separate idea followed by a pause.

Who has seen the wind? (pause)
Neither you nor I: (pause)
But when the trees bow down their
      heads (pause)
The wind is passing by.

> Christina Rossetti,
> "Who Has Seen the Wind?"

Another way is to pause at the punctuation in a line. In this stanza, then, the question mark at the end of line 1 indicates a pause, as does the colon at the end of line 2. In the third line, however, one could either pause after the word *heads* or read the last two lines as one long sentence. There is no right or wrong.

4. *Don't be afraid to make mistakes when you read poems aloud.* Everyone does. If you flub a reading, pick up and start again—this will help minimize the students' embarrassment when they make mistakes in their own readings. Both teacher and students can learn together.

5. *Read with your heart rather than your head.* If you wish to laugh as you read, do so. When a poem is sad, don't hide your sadness; let it enter your voice just as you would let happiness.

Children know what emotions are—do not underestimate their ability to know if you are reading with honesty. They would much rather have a flawed, sincere reading from you than the perfectly enunciated recitation on a tape or record.

Don't be afraid to make the leap. Leave your head in arithmetic, in history, in social studies, in science; and bring your heart and sense of delight to poetry! You may astound yourself; you will astound your students—and together you will begin a love for poetry that you may never before have imagined possible.

Myra Cohn Livingston, ODYSSEY's poetry consultant, is Poet-in-Residence for the Beverly Hills Unified School District and a Senior Instructor at UCLA Extension. The author of thirty books, she has received many awards for her poetry, including the National Council of Teachers of English Award for Excellence in Poetry for Children, which was awarded her in 1980.

Bibliography

Books About Poetry

Ciardi, John. *How Does a Poem Mean?* Boston: Houghton Mifflin, 1959.

Hughes, Ted. *Poetry Is.* New York: Doubleday, 1970.

Kennedy, X. J. *An Introduction to Poetry.* 4th ed. Boston: Little, Brown, 1978.

Individual Poets

Bodecker, N. M. *Hurry, Hurry, Mary Dear! and Other Nonsense Poems.* New York: Atheneum, 1976.

Gasztold, Carmen Bernos de. *Prayers from the Ark.* New York: Viking Press, 1962.

Giovanni, Nikki. *Spin a Soft Black Song.* London: Leonard Hill Books, 1971.

Hughes, Langston. *Don't You Turn Back.* New York: Alfred A. Knopf, 1969.

Kennedy, X. J. *The Phantom Ice Cream Man: More Nonsense Verse.* New York: Atheneum, 1979.

Merriam, Eve. *Finding a Poem.* New York: Atheneum, 1970.

Moore, Lilian. *Think of Shadows.* New York: Atheneum, 1980.

Sandburg, Carl. *Wind Song.* New York: Harcourt, Brace, 1960.

Silverstein, Shel. *Where the Sidewalk Ends.* New York: Harper & Row, 1974.

Starbird, Kaye. *Don't Ever Cross a Crocodile.* Philadelphia: J. B. Lippincott, 1963.

Worth, Valerie. *Still More Small Poems.* New York: Farrar, Straus & Giroux, 1978.

Anthologies

Behn, Harry, trans. *Cricket Songs.* New York: Harcourt Brace Jovanovich, 1964. Haiku attuned to young people.

Benedetti, Mario, ed. *Unstill Life: An Introduction to the Spanish Poetry of Latin America.* Translated by Darwin J. Flakoll and Claribel Alegria. New York: Harcourt Brace & World, 1969.

Bierhorst, John, ed. *In the Trail of the Wind: American Indian Poems and Ritual Orations.* New York: Farrar, Straus & Giroux, 1971.

Bontemps, Arna, ed. *Hold Fast to Dreams: Poems Old and New.* Chicago: Follett, 1969. Poems by Black Americans.

Brewton, John E., and Blackburn, Lorraine A., comps. *They've Discovered a Head in the Box for the Bread and Other Laughable Limericks.* New York: Harper & Row, 1978.

Livingston, Myra Cohn, ed. *O Frabjous Day! Poetry for Holidays and Special Occasions.* New York: Atheneum, 1978.

Mackay, David, ed. *A Flock of Words: An Anthology of Poetry for Children and Others.* New York: Harcourt Brace Jovanovich, 1970. A splendid collection for middle grades and older readers.

Folk Literature and the Teacher

Barre Toelken

'Twas on a Thursday evening
late in the fall of the year. The
weather was wild outside. Rain fell
and the wind blew till the walls of
the cottage shook. There they all
sat around the fire, busy with this
thing and that. But all at once,
something gave three taps on the
windowpane — tap! tap! tap!

> *East O' the Sun and
> West O' the Moon,* a
> Norwegian folk tale

SOMETIMES, in our rush to expose students to the best and most lasting examples of literature, we strive to present all the famous and well-known authors without recognizing that our students, and we ourselves, already come equipped with a fund of literary experience learned from our own families, friends, regional and ethnic groups. Even though the word *literature* is based on a Latin term meaning "letters" or "writing," the creation of stories, rituals, poetry, songs, drama, and games is as old as humankind itself: only in the most recent few minutes on history's clock has literary expression had much to do directly with the written word. But just as the ancient Greeks recited poems about epic adventures of centuries past, we continue oral traditions today as we tell jokes, legends, proverbs, riddles, and tales, using figures of speech and slang and varying our vocal tones to indicate such abstractions as sarcasm,

parody, love, stress, and commitment. In other words, much of the *quality* of our expressions, much of the *feel* of situations that bring us to laughter or give voice to our anxieties, continue to be expressed orally and often in the shared, inherited forms we call *folklore.*

Folklore provides a broad and complex field of study, but for practical purposes we can say that it is made up of informally learned beliefs, customs, mores, expressions, gestures, and observances that we come to know not through the formal channels of education, but by everyday associations with the people closest to us. We do not learn these primarily through print or other official channels; rather, they come to us in the jokes we hear from our families and friends, the gestures we pick up from those around us, the customs we use at birthday parties and religious holidays, the foods we eat at festival times, the lullabies we sing to our children, and the games we learn from each other. Folklore is also made up of the different narrative forms it takes as it is passed along: riddles, jingles, counting-out rhymes, folk songs, jump-rope rhymes, folk tales, legends, myths, and fables. The word *folklore,* then, simply refers to any traditions that people actually share, perform, or recall.

An important element in every type of folklore is the use of repetition. We find repetition in all literature, of course, but written literature tends to reduce or hide it in order to avoid redundancy, while folklore tends to emphasize it in order to produce a more recognizable structure and sense of direction. In northern Europe and among European Americans, the most common organizational and structural device is the use of three-part repetition. We look forward to the third occurrence because we know that something different or important will happen there. For example, the glass slipper in *Cinderella* cannot really fit the foot of the first sister, for it would destroy all our expectations, get rid of suspense, and make the story pointless. The key thing to remember is that different cultures use different kinds of repetition. Some, like many Native American tribes and several cultures in Asia, use a four-way repetition, which suggests a circle of the four directions instead of a linear movement toward a surprise ending. A few groups, like many of the Pacific Northwest Indian tribes, use the number five to suggest a cluster of stability (five villages, five chiefs, five adventures). We must always look for the way repetition is actually employed in folklore before we can see beyond the repeated patterns into the unstated assumptions of the culture whose game, legend, myth, or folk tale we and our students seek to understand.

Because folklore is transmitted orally, it "takes form" when it is actually being shared—when someone tells a story or a joke, when children jump rope, or when we sing "Happy Birthday to You" to someone. We can always learn something by looking beyond the words and into the situation where they come to life. Thus we understand the meaning of a folk expression only when we understand its context, including the customs and values which are its cultural "surroundings."

One important function of folklore is that it helps us reexperience and demonstrate the depth of connection with our closest groups. In some societies, the individual is encouraged to become quite independent from family and culture. At the same time, this very independence can be loaded with emotional uncertainty, alienation, and even fear. Folklore traditions compensate for the potential isolation an individual might feel by supplying a surrounding of familiar, shared values and expressions that make cultural life meaningful and stable. In other cultures, folk traditions are precisely what bind individuals together into a functioning group.

Beyond this, there is a practical reason for including a serious look at folklore in any introduction to literature: our students and we ourselves already know what's going on in it. Since our students already know and use counting and jump-rope rhymes, jokes, and word games, it should not be difficult to engage them in meaningful conversations about context, meaning, and usage—matters that, after all, not only help them understand their own expressions better but might well serve as a way of presenting written literature as closely related to what they already know. Students who can recognize metaphors in their own speech are less likely to find the metaphors of others strange. Instead of fighting the use of slang, we can profitably discuss it to see what it accomplishes. (What we find is that slang often does the same thing that poetry does: it says things with more power.) We can probe with our students which slang terms are powerful and which ones are not.

Students who see that their own jokes and games have structure and meaning will be more aware of structure and meaning in other kinds of literature. Students can easily talk about jump-rope games and rhymes in terms of structure, word play, and rhythms as well as the way they parody stock situations in the adult world and in their own. Customs determining who gets to keep a found object, who may go first in a game, who must be "it," as well as customs determining "correct" behavior in the group, are all expressed with specific traditional phrases, many of which use rhyme or metaphor. Ask students to discuss "dibs," "finders keepers," and the like, and it will be more natural to move to a discussion of word play, rhythm, metaphor, parody, and expressive joy in all literature.

Too often we assume that "real literature" is so far beyond our students that they cannot possibly understand its meanings and styles. A discussion of their own folklore, should help them see that literary expression is not foreign to the experience of ordinary human beings.

Indeed, many of the most powerful and lasting pieces of literature in all languages have been based on the topics, structures, and styles of oral literature, and many of them existed first as oral literature long before they were written down. We think of *Beowulf,* the *Iliad,* the *Odyssey, El Cid,* the Yugoslav epics, the English and Scottish popular, or folk, ballads, and the great, powerful myths of all major cultures. We recall, too, that Willa Cather, Chaucer, Shakespeare, T. S. Eliot, George Eliot, Langston Hughes, and others too numerous to mention have utilized folklore in their works to gain the tremendous literary power that comes from using familiar references to worlds of perception they and their audiences were already immersed in, their shared sense of reality, their concepts of the human cultural situation, that they learned from childhood onward.

As teachers, we can help students recognize, rather than avoid, these culturally shaped resources, these familiar codes that they themselves may apply to the deeper perception and enjoyment of literature. Students can more easily see the relationship between themselves and literature when they can see and hear what they have in common with poets—and that makes one fine place to start.

Barre Toelken is director of the Folklore and Ethnic Studies Program and professor of English at the University of Oregon. A Fulbright Research Professor in 1979–80 and a past president of the American Folklore Society, Dr. Toelken is a consultant on folklore for the National Endowment for the Arts, as well as a consultant on Native American culture for school districts throughout the country.

Bibliography

Professional Readings in Folklore

Brunvand, Jan Harold. *The Study of American Folklore.* 2d ed. New York: W. W. Norton, 1978. This basic textbook on folklore genres in America has separate descriptive and illustrative chapters on folk tales, myths, folk songs, customs, games, crafts, and so on.

Knapp, Mary, and Knapp, Herbert. *One Potato, Two Potato: The Folklore of American Children.* New York: W. W. Norton, 1978.

Opie, Iona, and Opie, Peter. *The Lore and Language of School Children.* London: Oxford University Press, 1959.

Toelken, Barre. *The Dynamics of Folklore.* Boston: Houghton Mifflin, 1979.

Folklore Anthologies for Children

Emrich, Duncan. *The Hodgepodge Book.* New York: Four Winds Press, 1972.

Lomax, Alan. *The Folk Songs of North America.* Garden City, N.Y.: Dolphin Books, 1975.

Thompson, Stith, ed. *One Hundred Favorite Folktales.* Bloomington, Ind.: Indiana University Press, 1968.

Resource Center

About the Authors and Illustrators

These notes present some information about the authors and illustrators in this book upon whom material was available.

Babbitt, Natalie See page 293 of the pupil's textbook.

Behn, Harry Harry Behn was born in 1898 in a mining camp near an Indian reservation. "Nothing has ever meant more to me than the lore I learned as a child from the Indians" he has said. He later moved from Arizona to Connecticut, where he began writing for children. He has written a number of stories and poems for children and has translated several books of Japanese haiku.

Carroll, Lewis (1832–1898) This was the pen name used by Charles Dodgson, the author of *Alice's Adventures in Wonderland* and its sequel *Through the Looking Glass.* Mr. Dodgson was a mathematics teacher at Christ Church College in Oxford, England. Because he stammered throughout his life, Mr. Dodgson never felt at ease with other adults. He much preferred the company of children. His *Alice* books grew out of the tales he told to young Alice Liddell and her two sisters. Many of the poems in these fantasy tales are humorous imitations of works of serious poets.

Coatsworth, Elizabeth As a child Elizabeth Coatsworth visited Europe, Egypt, and several regions of the United States with her family. She has continued to travel throughout her life, and her experiences have enabled her to write stories about people living in such diverse places as Guatemala, Greenland, France, and the West Indies. Now living in a red farmhouse in the state of Maine, Elizabeth Coatsworth says that she only writes about subjects that excite her: "Subjects are like sauce pans; you have to find the handle to use one."

Cohen, Barbara When asked how she got started as a writer, Barbara Cohen said, "I think I'm a writer because I spent my childhood listening to my relatives tell stories about each other. I don't write the stories they told, but I absorbed atmosphere and the tale-telling habit from them." Many of Ms. Cohen's books are about children living in the New York–New Jersey area, where she grew up.

Eager, Edward Though a playwright and lyricist by profession, Edward Eager began writing books for children to entertain his son Fritz. His characters in *Half Magic* were modeled on children he knew. He says, "When I was eight-to-twelve, I lived across from a family of three girls who are . . . the prototypes for Jane and Katharine and Martha. . . ."

Fleischman, Sid See page 403 of the pupil's textbook for the feature about this author.

Fritz, Jean Jean Fritz is best known for her series of books about great Americans of the colonial and revolutionary periods. Her books are remarkable for their liveliness as well as their historical accuracy. Interestingly enough, Jean Fritz, who writes so well about America's history, was not born in the United States: she was born halfway around the world, in Hankow, China.

Frost, Robert (1874–1963)   Robert Frost is considered by many to be America's greatest poet. He was born in San Francisco, California, in 1874, but grew up in New England. Frost married a high school classmate and went to Harvard University for two years. He left college to farm thirty acres in New Hampshire and to write poetry. Frost remained unknown and unpublished until he moved his family to England in 1912. His first two books of poetry, published in England, were popular, and he returned to America three years later, known and admired. During his life, he won the Pulitzer Prize for his poetry four times.

George, Jean Craighead   Jean Craighead George says, "I write about children in nature and their relationship to the complex web of life of which we are but one small part." Though she began her career as a newspaper reporter, she has been writing novels about nature for more than thirty years.

Greene, Bette   Because Bette Greene came from a background unlike that of the other children in the Arkansas Delta town where she grew up, she felt different and alone during much of her childhood. Her first book, *Summer of My German Soldier,* tells about a girl with similar feelings. Bette Greene herself says that childhood sights, smells, and memories are the basis for much of what she writes.

Heinlein, Robert   As one of the pioneers of juvenile science fiction, Robert Heinlein took a lonely step forward in 1947

when he wrote his first book for young adults *Rocket Ship Galileo.* But the adventure of teenagers who fly to the moon caught the attention of both readers and reviewers. His novel now marks the first time science fiction became a recognized branch of children's literature.

Hughes, Langston (1902–1967)   Langston Hughes began writing poetry in high school and had his first poem published shortly after he graduated. That poem, "The Negro Speaks of Rivers," is one of his most popular. During his long career as a writer, Hughes produced several volumes of poetry, as well as fiction, plays, newspaper columns, and autobiographical works.

Hughes, Ted   English poet and novelist Ted Hughes believes that "Poets write poems to amuse themselves, partly." He has written *Poetry Is,* an informal introduction to poetry for young readers; *Nessie, The Mannerless Monster; Moon-Whales and Other Poems;* and many other works for children.

Konigsburg, E. L.   See page 31 of the pupil's textbook for the feature about this author.

Krumgold, Joseph   Because his father built theaters, young Joseph Krumgold became very interested in making movies. Not long after graduating from college, he set out for Hollywood. He later became a writer and producer of documentary films.
. . . *And Now, Miguel* was based on what Joseph Krumgold learned while working on a documentary film about the Navajo people.

Kuskin, Karla   See page 207 of the pupil's textbook for the feature about this poet.

Lear, Edward (1812–1888)   Englishman Edward Lear was the youngest of twenty-one children. He became a highly skilled landscape painter, but Lear got his greatest joy from pleasing young people with his humorous verses and drawings. The first of his *Nonsense Books* began as a present for the child of one of the people who supported his work as an artist.

Lewis, C. S. (1899–1963)   C. S. Lewis was an author who wrote many popular fantasy stories as well as important scholarly works. Lewis taught at universities in England for more than thirty years. During that time, he wrote science fiction and fantasy, such as the seven-volume *Chronicles of Narnia.* When asked for advice about writing, C. S. Lewis replied, in part, "1. Turn off the radio. 2. Read all the good books you can, and avoid nearly all magazines. 3. Always write (and read) with the ear, not the eye. You should hear every sentence you write as if it was being read aloud or spoken. If it does not sound nice, try again. 4. Write about what really interests you, whether it is real things or imaginary things, and nothing else . . . ." C. S. Lewis died in 1963 at the age of 64.

Livingston, Myra Cohn   Myra Cohn Livingston was once a professional French horn player, but most of her career has been devoted to writing poetry and helping young people learn to write poetry. Besides publishing eight volumes of her own poetry, she has edited seven volumes of poetry and has written a book for teachers about teaching poetry-writing. She has also taught many classes and workshops for young people, teachers, and the general public.

Lopez, Alonzo   See page 235 of the pupil's textbook for the feature about this poet.

Merriam, Eve   Eve Merriam's poetry is an exciting way to explore the everyday world. Eve Merriam wants people to enjoy poetry. She has said, "When something is too beautiful or too terrible or even too funny for words: then it is time for poetry." Eve Merriam is well known for her poetry books *Catch a Little Rhyme, It Doesn't Always Have to Rhyme,* and *There Is No Rhyme for Silver.*

O'Dell, Scott   See page 341 of the pupil's textbook for the feature about this author.

Roethke, Theodore /ret′·kē/   Theodore Roethke grew up in Saginaw, Michigan, where his father owned a greenhouse. Years later, the greenhouse and its plants and flowers were the subject of many of Theodore Roethke's poems. Theodore Roethke was awarded a Pulitzer Prize in 1954 for his book of poems *The Waking.*

Schwartz, Alvin   Alvin Schwartz first became interested in folklore when a child. He enjoyed knowing and telling all the jokes, riddles, and silly songs that were popular. At that time, he says, he never realized that "these games, songs, jokes, tales, and customs were often very old, that ordinary people like me had created them."

Sealth, Chief   Chief Sealth led the Duwamish and Suquamish tribes of the Puget Sound region in a policy of friendship toward settlers in the 1850s. He lived to see the settlement of Seattle, which was named for him, become a bustling city.

Selden, George   Like Chester Cricket, George Selden grew up in Connecticut but moved to New York City. He says that he got the idea for *The Cricket in Times Square* late one night when he was in the Times Square subway station and heard a cricket chirp. In 1973 this popular book was made into a half-hour animated TV program, which is reshown periodically.

Serraillier, Ian   Ian Serraillier was a schoolmaster in England for twenty-five years. He has published more than forty-four books, including books of poetry and modern adventure stories. He also has re-told many classical myths and legends. Mr. Serraillier explains, "it is to Greece and Rome and early English literature that I have mainly turned. I have sought out the best stories—however hard one tries, one could never improve on the stories that have stood the test of time . . ."

Smith, Moyne Rice   All of Moyne Rice Smith's careers and interests have pointed her toward the writing of plays. She was a teacher of English and dramatics, an ac-tress, and a director of children's drama groups and her own summer theater. She also founded a drama group, the Princeton (New Jersey) Junior Community Players.

Snyder, Zilpha Keatley   See page 255 of the pupil's textbook for the feature about this author.

Stuart, Jesse   Jesse Stuart was born in a one-room log cabin in the hill country of Kentucky. He did not attend school regu-larly until he was fifteen because he was needed to work on his family's farm. He then went through high school and worked his way through college to become a high school teacher. At that time, he began writ-ing poems, stories, and articles about life in his part of Kentucky.

Thurber, James (1894–1961)   Losing the sight of one eye as a child did not stop James Thurber from drawing cartoons, writ-ing fables, inventing improbable characters, and generally delighting Americans from the mid-1920s until his death in 1961. Much of Thurber's work was published in *The New Yorker* magazine. His best-known short story, "The Secret Life of Walter Mitty," has become an American classic.

Travers, P. L.   Pamela Travers began writing *Mary Poppins* when she was in a 900-year-old English country house recov-ering from an illness. Because a friend showed interest in the stories, she contin-ued writing, and a series of five Mary Pop-pins books resulted.

Professional Resources for the Teacher

Baskin, Barbara H., and Harris, Karen H. *Books for the Gifted Child.* New York: R. R. Bowker, 1980. An annotated list of almost 150 books for gifted children from kindergarten to upper grades, ac-companied by several chapters on the historical and social problems of the gifted child.

Cianciolo, Patricia Jean, ed. *Picture Books for Children.* Chicago: American Library Association, 1973. This list of picture books is annotated with story synopses and art critiques. Categories of interest include Me and My Family, Other Peo-ple, The World I Live In, and The Imagi-native World.

Cullinan, Bernice E., et al. *Literature and the Child.* New York: Harcourt Brace Jovanovich, 1981. Along with selections of outstanding books, this book dis-cusses criteria in choosing books for children and presents many practical teaching ideas.

Huck, Charlotte S. *Children's Literature in the Elementary School.* 3d rev. ed. New York: Holt, Rinehart & Winston, 1979. A reliable, comprehensive aid for under-standing children's literature, for becom-ing familiar with classic and contempo-rary books, and for using books in the classroom.

Larrick, Nancy. *A Parent's Guide to Chil-dren's Reading.* 4th rev. ed. New York: Doubleday, 1975. An annotated listing of recommended books.

Livingston, Myra Cohn. *When You Are Alone / It Keeps You Capone: An Approach to Creative Writing with Children.* New York: Atheneum, 1973.

Lukens, Rebecca J. *A Critical Handbook of Children's Literature.* Glenview, Ill.: Scott, Foresman, 1976. Discusses the elements used to evaluate all literature—character, plot, setting, theme, point of view, style, and tone—and relates them to examples from children's books.

Moffett, James, and Wagner, Betty J. *Student Centered Language Arts and Reading, K–13: A Handbook for Teachers.* 2nd. ed. Boston: Houghton Mifflin, 1976.

Recommended Reading for the Student

Most of the books recommended in this bibliography are available in hardcover. Some materials, however, are listed as paperbacks because they were originally published in that form or because a hardcover version was not available for review. All of the books are divided into the categories of **easy, average,** and **challenging,** which indicate the reading levels of these books.

Easy

Cusack, Isabel Langis. *Mr. Wheatfield's Loft.* New York: Holt, Rinehart and Winston, 1981. Eleven-year-old Ellis Hampton befriends Mr. Wheatfield, who teaches him about racing pigeons, and by doing so, brings courage to a boy who is unable to speak.

Pinkwater, Daniel. *Attila the Pun: A Magic Moscow Book.* New York: Four Winds Press, 1981. When Norman, his boss

Steve, and a mystic seer conjure a fifth-century punster, their plans are turned topsy-turvy.

Viorst, Judith. *Alexander, Who Used to Be Rich Last Sunday.* New York: Atheneum, 1978. How Anthony and Nicholas and Alexander spent more than they bargained for. Sequel to *Alexander and the Terrible, Horrible, No Good, Very Bad Day.*

Average

Ainsworth, Ruth. *The Phantom Fisherboy: Tales of Mystery and Magic.* New York: Elsevier-Dutton, 1980. Ghosts, including a cat ghost, are featured in this collection of eighteen brief tales, suitable for telling as well as reading aloud.

Brewton, Sara and John. *Laughable Limericks.* New York: Thomas Y. Crowell, 1965.

Carrick, Carol. *Sand Tiger Shark.* New York: Houghton Mifflin, Seabury Press, 1977. This nonfiction book examines the life cycle of one sand tiger shark, including its biological makeup and hunting and eating patterns.

Emrich, Duncan. *The Hodgepodge Book.* New York: Four Winds Press, 1972. Almost every topic of interest to children is covered in this collection of knock-knock jokes, jump-rope rhymes, and riddles.

————. *The Nonsense Book of Riddles, Rhymes, Tongue Twisters, Puzzles, and Jokes from American Folklore.* New York: Four Winds Press, 1970.

Fritz, Jean. *Where Do You Think You're Going, Christopher Columbus?* New York: G. P. Putnam, 1980. A readable biography that provides insights into the character of a persistent explorer.

George, Jean Craighead. *My Side of the Mountain.* New York: E. P. Dutton, 1959. A boy learns to fend for himself in the wilderness of the Catskill Mountains.

_____. *All Upon a Sidewalk*. New York: E. P. Dutton, 1974. Searching for food, an ant takes a long, adventurous journey—all upon a sidewalk.

_____. *Hook a Fish, Catch a Mountain*. New York: E. P. Dutton, 1975. Spinner, a girl from New York City, is introduced to the wilderness by her cousin.

Griffin, Judith Berry. *Phoebe and the General*. New York: Coward, McCann & Geoghegan, 1977. During the Revolutionary War, Phoebe acts as a spy hoping to discover who would attempt to assassinate General George Washington.

Lear, Edward. *The Book of Nonsense, Reproduction of the 1846 Edition*. New York: Garland, 1976.

Lewis, C. S. *The Lion, the Witch and the Wardrobe: A Story for Children*. New York: Macmillan, 1950. While playing in a country house, four children discover that a wardrobe is an entrance into the magical world of Narnia. This book is the first title in the series "Chronicles of Narnia," which includes *Prince Caspian, The Voyage of the "Dawn Treader," The Silver Chair, The Horse and His Boy, The Magician's Nephew,* and *The Last Battle*.

Livingston, Myra Cohn. *A Lollygag of Limericks*. New York: Atheneum, 1978.

O'Dell, Scott. *Island of the Blue Dolphins*. New York: Houghton Mifflin, 1960. Left on a deserted island for eighteen years, a girl learns to cope with her loneliness and to survive.

Perl, Lila. *Hunter's Stew and Hangtown Fry: What Pioneer America Ate and Why*. New York: Houghton Mifflin, Clarion, 1977. Nonfiction commentary on the eating habits of pioneers.

Phelps, Ethel Johnston, ed. *Tatterhood and Other Tales*. New York: The Feminist Press, 1978. Twenty-five folk tales and legends with clever and resourceful women as main characters.

Challenging

De Angeli, Marguerite. *The Door in the Wall*. New York: Doubleday, 1949. This action-filled Newbery award winner gives the reader a look at life in the Middle Ages and the struggles a young boy has in dealing with his disability.

Lear, Edward. *Nonsense Botany*. New York: Frederick Warne, 1927. More of Lear's nonsense poetry accompanied by his own line drawings.

Manning-Sanders, Ruth. *A Book of Witches*. New York: E. P. Dutton, 1965. Twelve stories presenting witches of all kinds.

Wilkins, Frances. *Wizards and Witches*. New York: Henry Z. Walck, 1965. A simply explained history of magic and wizardry.

Related Media

The following key is used to identify the media listed below: **C**—cassette; **F**—film; **FS**—filmstrip; **R**—record. The catalog number immediately following each title should be used when ordering from the company identified in the entry.

Carroll, Lewis. *The Walrus and the Carpenter* and *Jabberwocky*. JFS 172 Old Greenwich, CT: Listening Library. **FS** with cassette.

Lewis, C. S. *The Chronicles of Narnia: The Lion, the Witch and the Wardrobe*. **R**—TC 1587 or **C**—CDL 51587 New York: Caedmon.

Thurber, James. *The Great Quillow*. **R**—TC 1411 or **C**—CDL 51411 New York: Caedmon.

Travers, P. L. *Mary Poppins*. **R**—TC 1246 or **C**—CDL 51246 New York: Caedmon.